*Paul & Jennifer Azzopardi
Azzopaedi Insurance Brokers*

INSURANCE
MARKETING

Y0-CBS-504

Arthur Meidan

Graham Burn
28d High Street
Leighton Buzzard
Bedfordshire
LU7 7EA
United Kingdom

In memory of my Father

First Published: January 1984
© *Arthur Meidan*

No part of this book may be reproduced, stored in a retrieval system or transmitted in any form, by any means, electronic, mechanical, photocopying, microfilming, recording or otherwise, without the written permission of the publisher.

ISBN 0 907721 16 8

Published & Printed by:
GRAHAM BURN
28d High Street
Leighton Buzzard
Bedfordshire
LU7 7EA
Tel: Leighton Buzzard (0525) 377963
Telex: 825562 CHACOM G BURNPUB

Typesetting & Artwork:
Graham Burn
Advertising Studios

PREFACE

The original inspiration for this book came from three sources. Firstly, I had substantial experience of teaching insurance marketing to practitioners in this industry through post-experience courses and seminars in Western Europe, the Middle East and South America. This experience identified a gap in the literature: there are indeed very few books on insurance marketing. The existent publications, mainly North American, are either general, dealing with *principles* of insurance (referring only indirectly to certain marketing aspects) or they concentrate on the *selling* of insurance. On many occasions, the delegates and participants on these seminars and courses have asked for a basic, non-technical book that presents, explains and describes the main marketing management processes in the insurance sector.

The second spur to the writing of this book was clear evidence of a need for a basic text that can be used by students taking the professional examinations of the Chartered Insurance Institute and the other professional organisations, such as the British Insurance Brokers Association or the College of Insurance.

Finally, in the last few years there has been an immense growth of interest in the marketing of financial services in general and of insurance marketing in particular. This increase in interest has resulted in the development of undergraduate courses on the marketing of financial services at a number of universities (e.g. City University Business School, Nottingham University, U.C.N.W. at Bangor and Sheffield University), at leading polytechnics (e.g. The City of London Polytechnic, The Polytechnic of Central London and Liverpool Polytechnic) and at some major colleges of technology such as The Glasgow College of Technology.

The structure of this book is intended to mirror the marketing functions and processes, as viewed through the eyes of insurance companies. The emphasis of the book is practical, although due attention is given to the theoretical foundations of marketing and their applicability to the insurance industry. Although the text deals mainly with general insurance (i.e. property, pecuniary and liability), a significant part of this book is devoted to the marketing of life assurance.

This book recognises that the major function of the insurance marketer is decision making. It focuses, therefore, on the major types of decision – and problems – facing the insurance marketing executive in his attempt to harmonise the objectives of the insurance company with the environment and opportunities found in the market place.

PREFACE

The first three chapters are introductory, presenting the special characteristics and factors affecting the insurance market — how an insurance company should develop and implement the marketing concept (as opposed to the sales approach) and its marketing programme. In order to develop a marketing programme, insurance customer behaviour and market segmentation should be thoroughly investigated. This is discussed in the following chapters. Next, marketing research methods and their roles in market segmentation and customer behaviour analysis are introduced. Based on the behaviour of the insurance market targets and the insurance company's own objectives, a marketing mix is developed emphasising product development strategies, principles of product innovation, pricing and ratemaking methods, advertising, promotion, selling and channels of distribution. Due to the critical importance of the selling function, a separate chapter investigates the issue of insurance salesforce management, including the selection, training and supervision of insurance salespersons and agents.

Finally, the last three chapters discuss the main elements of insurance marketing strategy, organisation, planning and control. The book concludes with a summary of recent developments and future trends in insurance marketing, including the roles of consumerism, customer protection regulation in this industry and the impact of inflation on insurance marketing operations.

In preparing this book I have accumulated debts to many.

I am grateful to Professor C. Arthur Williams Jnr., Editor of *The Journal of Risk and Insurance* (U.S.A.) for his permission to use and reproduce some of the material from an article by me originally published in that journal.

I am also grateful to Professor G. Clayton of Sheffield University for his encouragement and support in my endeavour to write this text and to my colleagues, Johnnie Peirson and Duncan Kitchin, for their valuable comments. Of course, none of these persons is responsible for the faults which remain and which are entirely my own responsibility.

Finally, I am indebted to my secretary, Miss Rebecca Jackson, for typing this manuscript and to my wife and family who have provided me with the time, support and inspiration needed to write this book.

Arthur Meidan, Ph.D.
Sheffield University
October 1983

CONTENTS

Preface iii

List of Tables vi

List of Figures vi

Introduction vii

Chapter 1: Special Characteristics and Factors Affecting the Marketing of Insurance. 1

Chapter 2: The Marketing Versus the Sales Concept in Insurance 9

Chapter 3: Developing the Insurance Marketing Programme 15

Chapter 4: Types of Market Segmentation 25

Chapter 5: Marketing Research 31

Chapter 6: Product Development 43

Chapter 7: Pricing 59

Chapter 8: Advertising and Promotions 71

Chapter 9: Channels of Distribution 81

Chapter 10: Sales Force Management 93

Chapter 11: Marketing Strategies in Insurance 115

Chapter 12: Marketing Organisation and Control 125

Chapter 13: Recent Developments and Future Trends in Insurance Marketing 135

Conclusions 145

References 147

Index 153

LIST OF TABLES

Table 1: The United Kingdom Personal Insurance Market — Consumer Incidence 4
Table 2: Life Insurance Segmentation 22
Table 3: The Variables Affecting Insurance Selection Criteria 36
Table 4: Non- parametric (Spearman) Correlation Coefficients of Attitudes on Insurance Selection 38
Table 5: Main Properties of Insurance Products 46
Table 6: Planning Insurance Product Strategies 57
Table 7: Characteristics of the Various Promotional Channels in Insurance 72
Table 8: Optimising Sales Time Allocation by Considering Both Customer Type and Product Group(s) 100
Table 9: Determinants of Success for Insurance Agents 106
Table 10: Quantitative and Descriptive Methods of Evaluating Insurance 110
Table 11: Insurance Salespersons' Performance Index 113
Table 12: Marketing Strategies in Insurance 116
Table 13: Criteria for Appraising Marketing Performance in an Insurance Company 132

LIST OF FIGURES

Figure 1: The Hazards Generating the Need for Insurance Marketing 3
Figure 2: The Marketing Approach System 11
Figure 3: The Insurance Marketing Programme 16
Figure 4: The Insurance Marketing Mix 20
Figure 5: Insurance Buying Behaviour 23
Figure 6: Criteria for Insurance Selection — A Profile Analysis 39
Figure 7: Conventional Life Assurance Products 44
Figure 8: The Insurance Product Life Cycle 51
Figure 9: The Major Methods of Insurance Pricing 63
Figure 10: Some Major Promotional Goals in Insurance 75
Figure 11: Direct vs Indirect Distribution Channels in Insurance 83
Figure 12: The Four Main Distinctive Stages in Selling Insurance 109
Figure 13: Insurance Marketing Strategy Plan 121
Figure 14: Typical Insurance Marketing Department Organisation 126
Figure 15: Types of Marketing Control in an Insurance Organisation 129
Figure 16: Recent and Future Trends in Insurance Marketing 138

INTRODUCTION

As the role of the insurance sector continues to grow in the economies of most of the western nations, pressures are mounting for more effective marketing management of the services offered by the insurance companies. Insurance is a financial service industry which has recently been transformed by aggressive competitive tendencies. For this reason, in the last few years there has been a growing interest in applying marketing techniques and tools in the field of insurance. This growing interest has generated a relatively large number of publications, mostly descriptive, in the last 4 – 5 years[1,2]. Along with this change in approach, has come a change in the insurance companies' marketing strategies and patterns of organisation and control, as elaborated below.

The 'revolution' in insurance marketing, mainly due to competition in products and pricing, has caused the industry to enter an era of accelerated change. This change has been boosted even more today by the industry's gigantic size. In the United States, for example, the total annual volume of corporate and personal insurance is around $260 billions, representing about 15% of all business and family expenditures. The insurance companies' assets exceed $500 billion and about 2% of the working population is employed in this industry. The United Kingdom, unlike the U.S.A., remains a country in which a high proportion of population is either underinsured or not insured at all. One of the reasons is that the marketing system for insurance is a multi-faceted one including both private and government (tax-supported) ones and, in this country, many risks and catastrophes are covered by the state social security system. However, still it is an important growing sector with over $5 billion (£2.7 billion) yearly premiums for life assurance and annuities alone, in 1974[3]. Indeed, governments, through laws and regulations, create a 'need' for insurance. In many countries, it is now a legal requirement that motorists should have an insurance cover for their liability to third parties. The situation may also arise between individuals or institutions, such as commercial banks, requiring their customers to insure imported goods which are being paid for through a letter of credit. Building societies, hire purchase companies and principals in construction contracts also impose a requirement for an insurance cover. Insurance contracts embody the principles of insurable interest and utmost good faith, the purpose of which is to eliminate the possibility that society will be prejudiced by the insurance product. Insurers are also required to reduce the incidence of loss and of economic waste by encouraging prevention measures and safety precautions. If such aims are not pursued sufficiently, the product can be priced beyond the financial capabilities of many, which may not be in the interest of the public.

Insurance may be termed as a quasi-collective service. It is characterised by significant external economies. The price paid by one individual has a spill-over effect which may generate benefits to others. Insurance in essence is a subsidy created by the many, who are subject to a certain risk, to the few, who are affected by the occurrence of the risk. Such a characteristic creates situations which the marketer of insurance has to take into consideration in his efforts to satisfy the consumer[4].

The identification and satisfaction of customer needs is the focus of marketing activities of most insurance companies. These objectives could be attained through the identification of possible marketing mix strategies and their outcomes. There are several types of insurance service. The major two categories are: general insurance and life assurance. This text deals with both categories, although it concentrates on general insurance (i.e. the property, pecuniary and liability aspects of the industry).

The present life assurance companies, however, have moved from being ones that are solely life companies offering a few services, to providing and presenting themselves to be full financial service institutions. A life assurance company can be looked upon in two separate and distinct ways. First of all, it is a company that provides a means of protecting against death or sickness, or as an investment company for savings. The second view is that the company provides a service for the public with all the necessary back-up and after sales service. The back-up includes, as well as insurance investment performance, claims settlement and other contractual benefits and a life assurance advisory service for the public.

The selling of life assurance is very competitive and marketing is, in fact, the most important factor affecting the overall level of business. However, it is beset by many problems due to the uncompetitive premium rates and the fact that new products cannot be used as a form of competition. In brief, the life assurance industry has tried to identify and classify the different markets available to create a variety of products to meet the needs of the potential customers and to suit their income groups. In this respect, life assurance companies are no different from general insurance companies.

The term "life insurance" can be defined in terms of benefits. The three most important ones are[5]:

1. *A whole life insurance* refers to the fixed sum to be paid to the beneficiary at the time of the death of the insured, regardless of when it occurs;

2. *Term life assurance* is the same as 1. above provided, however, that the death will occur within a *limited* period;

3. *Endowment insurance* provides for the payment of a benefit:

    i) in the event of death of the insured within a certain period (the "endowment period"); *or*,

    ii) at the end of the endowment period (provided the insured is living).

The market for life assurances is not homogeneous and segmentation has occurred to a significant extent. Indeed, many subsidiary companies have been established by the insurance firms, because of the great market potential within the life assurance business and group pensions.

The savings type life policies are composed of both protection and savings elements. Consequently, rational customers for life assurances should first decide the value they place on the protection against premature death. On this basis the expected rate of return on premiums payable can be calculated.

In certain countries – including the U.K., but not the U.S.A. – life assurance policy holders receive income tax relief on premiums paid for these policies. As a result U.S.A. life insurance policies are more expensive than in the U.K. and generally most U.S. customers buy life assurance for protection, whilst U.K. customers are mainly interested in the saving aspects of life assurance.

CHAPTER ONE

SPECIAL CHARACTERISTICS AND FACTORS AFFECTING THE MARKETING OF INSURANCE

Unlike other products and services, the best an insurance company can do is to promise the customer that, by acquiring an insurance policy, he or she will be in a position no worse and no better than the situation existent before the event against which the service that has been provided has occurred. To the insurance customer, buying insurance means accepting relatively small, but definite financial loss in order to avoid a larger (probable) loss.

The special characteristics that make the marketing of insurance products distinctively different from the manufacturing ones are numerous.

a) *Perishability*

Most insurance products are direct (i.e. they cannot be inventoried). The perishability of insurance services leaves the insurance company manager without an important buffer that is available to manufacturing managers, so pricing (as well as other marketing tools, such as distribution, advertising and promotion) have a paramount importance and role.

b) *Inseparability*

There is a high degree of insurer/insured interaction in the production and offering of the insurance cover which is a mixed blessing: while the consumers are indeed a source of productive capacity, their role creates uncertainty for managers about the quality of their services and the accommodation of the needs of the consumers and, therefore, the need to bring the consumer into contact with the service delivery system (or the system to the consumer). This characteristic might drastically affect pricing through the higher costs of providing an effective localised insurance distribution system and/or substantial spending on advertising and promotion in order to bring the consumer to the insurance delivery outlet.

c) *Heterogenity*

Most insurance products are very heterogenic. Since over 15% of *all* business and family expenditures in the U.S.A. are spent on corporate and personal insurances[6], the level of services differentiation — and, therefore, of competition is very great indeed[7]. For this reason, pricing (as well as the other marketing mix tools) has an important role to play, *especially* on those insurance products that have reached the maturity stage of their life cycle (e.g. individual or motor insurance).

d) *Fluctuations in Demand*

Fluctuations in demand in certain (but not all) types of insurance is even more important than in product markets; the demand for these insurance services is fairly elastic (i.e. a substantial increase/decrease in personal disposable income often leads to sharp changes in demand, leading to intense competition and the need to use the price tool). Also, accelerating advances in technological sophistication, as well as social and competitive changes continually reshape the existing insurance markets.

e) *Labour Intensive*

The insurance industry is labour intensive and is, therefore, generally more difficult to control than other industries, so it is very important to check on salesperson's performances and to try to economise on the use of personnel.

The need for insurance services arises because of the three types of system that create hazards and uncertainty* (figure 1):

1. The social system creates hazards such as burglary, arson, riots, civil commotion, strikes or kidnapping. This leaves the individual or an institution in the society in a state of financial uncertainty.

2. The natural system relates to those natural causes (or forces) which can cause fires, hurricanes, earthquakes, lightning, floods, storms, tempests and several other hazards.

3. The technical system (i.e. that created by individuals and institutions *within* a society) can create the hazards of fire, explosion, pollution, radiation, contamination, breakdown, collision, impact and various other hazards.

The natural risks are static in the sense that they do not change in nature, but only in intensity and frequency. On the basis of past experience, these hazards and risks can be calculated with a certain degree of accuracy. The social risks, on the other hand, are related to the activities of that society and are, therefore, changeable and more dynamic according to the changing characteristics of the society in which the insurance services are offered. The technical hazards are the easiest to predict, as they are functions of the technical activities (in relation to the environment) in the particular circumstances.

---

*The major types of systems that create hazards and uncertainty are further discussed in Sequeira, P.4: "The Marketing of Insurance", Ph.D. dissertation, University of Sheffield, (forthcoming 1984).

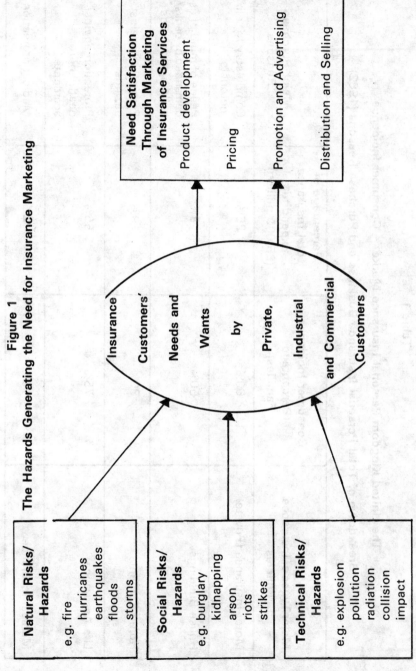

Figure 1

The Hazards Generating the Need for Insurance Marketing

Table 1

The United Kingdom Personal Insurance Market – Consumer Incidence

Breakdown of Total Personal Insurance Business and Purchase Reasons (1982)

Major Types of Insurance Policies	Consumer Incidence (Percentage Families)	Percentage of Total Insurance Expenditure (£5,000 million)	Major Purchase Reasons
Motor Insurance (Private)	60%	25%	Compulsory for all motorists
House Buildings	50%	8%	Peace of mind or as demanded by banks/ building societies
Home Contents	80%	9%	Protection against hazards
Life Assurance	75%	56%	Protection against death and/or accidents
Medical Insurance	10%	2%	Medical protection

f) *Pooling of Losses*

Pooling or sharing of losses is another basic aspect of the insurance. Pooling means that the actual loss is substituted for the average loss. The pooling aspect is based on the prediction of future average losses, based on large numbers of units/customers, so that accuracy is achieved.

g) *Risk Transfer*

A further characteristic of insurance is the payment of fortuitous losses (i.e. losses that are unforeseen and/or unexpected and are either accidental or the result of chance). This results in what is called risk transfer. This is an essential element of insurance. In fact, the risk is transferred from the insured to the insurer, who should be in a strong financial position, in order to meet and pay unexpected losses.

As can be seen from Table 1, consumer incidence of insurance is quite high, particularly in life and home contents insurance. The size of the market (more than £5,000 million expenditure in premium income in 1982 from the U.K. *personal sector* alone) has led to over 600 different U.K. and overseas insurance companies operating in this industry in the U.K., involving in addition about one hundred advertisers with a total insurance advertising expenditure in excess of £25 million (1982). Total U.K. insurance premiums amount to over 5% of the total GNP. (In the U.S.A. the net annual premiums in 1982 amounted to over $160 billion plus about $100 billion from government insurance programmes.[8]) The gigantic size of the industry today has led to tremendous competition in the insurance industry. In order to be able to compete successfully in the industry, insurers should attempt to design special plans (products) that are unique or almost so. Since product innovation is easily copied by other companies, one of the major roles of the insurance marketer is to suggest a "package" that precludes price comparisons with other companies' products.

Market competition in insurance has also attracted the interest of competent salespersons. Sales management, or "insuremanship", is now of major interest to most large insurers, attempting to attract the most efficient salespersons by competitive remuneration and inducements. According to Rejda[9], in the U.S.A. the incomes of insurance agents, particularly those selling life and health policies, range from $13,000 in the first year to those earning in excess of $150,000 per annum. In the U.K., agents' commissions as a percentage of premium income amounts to between 5.2% and 5.9%.

Factors Affecting the Insurance Market

Before insurance policies can be marketed and a marketing programme drawn up, the major factors that influence the market have to be considered. Obviously, the rapidly changing economy has a considerable influence on the demand for insurance products and services. There are six major influencing variables which have shaped out and characterise the marketing of insurance in the Western world today:

1) *The Impact of Legislation and Tax Concessions*

Legislative requirements and restrictions can exert a considerable influence on the size and scope of the market. This influence can take several forms, ranging from control of the number of offices operating in the market to the types of contract written or even to the detailed policy conditions. In many Western countries, however, these types of control are not enforced, so insurance companies have a relatively free hand in their operations, so long as all the basic legal requirements have been met.

In fact, in some ways, legislation actually aids the insurance industry in the form of tax concessions which encourage long-term savings (e.g. through life assurance policies). In certain countries (including the U.K.), relief from tax at the basic rate is granted on half the premium on life policies up to a maximum premium of a certain percentage of the total taxable income[10]. The method of taxation used has allowed pure life cover (i.e. protection) to be obtained at a very low cost, while the freedom from restrictions on investment policies has made it possible for policy holders to obtain good returns. Marketing of most life assurance policies in most of the free world countries has also been relatively free from legislation. There is relatively limited control in the formulation of contracts and in the granting of agencies, though the insurers have kept a close view on all new financial and insurance Acts to seize any opportunity for designing and implementing new policies at the right time to meet the public changing needs.

2) *Size and Distribution of the Population and National Income*

The size of the population might be expected to have a particular direct influence on the market for insurance and particularly life assurance. However, this is not necessarily true as other elements, such as the density and distribution of the population and demographic and socio-economic factors, should be taken into consideration as well.

When real income is increasing rapidly, there will be a tendency for personal consumption to increase. At the same time, personal savings will be channelled to the traditional financial institutions like banks and building societies, whilst some will be channelled to life assurance companies. This shows that there will be a large potential market for life assurance when national income increases. However, the major problem here is the competition from other financial institutions and the effects of inflation.

3) *Competition*

Aggressive competition and the increasing costs of service and administration have led, on the one hand, to the elimination of small unprofitable companies and, on the other hand, to difficulty in offering personal service. Thus, it became a trend for insurance companies to amalgamate in order to exploit the economies of scale and to invest heavily in computers and other ancillary equipments in order to:

a) calculate their cost accurately;

b) achieve lower operational costs; and,

c) expand their service capability.

In order to combat competition, wider cover for little or no extra premium (pricing policy) is now being offered. Other channels of distribution for reaching the public (e.g. by direct selling over the counter or mail orders with more economically packaged contracts) are being explored.

Savings can also be effected (as noted above) through banks and building societies which provide both long-term and short-term saving facilities. Life assurance policies are a form of long-term savings, but as most savers usually prefer to hold cash or short-term assets, the life companies are at a disadvantage. Furthermore, the severe bouts of inflation recently have also increased the reluctance of the public to enter into long-term financial commitments. So, insurance companies will have to find ways and means of drawing savers away from the traditional financial institutions, either by guaranteeing surrender values (i.e. the amount of money refunded when a policy holder cashes in his policy) or allowing the policy holder to borrow against the surrender value so that he knows his money is not completely tied up.

4) *Inflation*

Most of the free world has faced, and is still facing, certain inflation levels and high taxation which both reduce purchasing power. Many potential insurance customers who believed that inflation could or would be stopped completely were disillusioned, so there is now a growing awareness of the need to budget as well as to invest wisely. Accordingly, sales of assurances (and especially of the traditional whole life and endowment policy which was designed to provide for savings) declined. In its place, policies with an investment element attached, like endowment with profits, associated with unit trusts emerged, in order to maintain the future purchasing power of the insured. Inflation – even at moderate levels – will continue to influence insurance marketing, as elaborated in Chapter Thirteen.

5) *The Use of Mass Merchandising*
Lately, particularly in the U.S.A., the emphasis has been upon mass mechandising (i.e. a plan for insuring a number of otherwise independent risks under a single programme of insurance at a premium lower than that charged for similar protection to persons not participating in such plans, but with the insurer retaining the right of individual underwriting selection of participants). This provides for consumer groups to be used as indicators of their potential importance (e.g. employees of the same employer, members of trade unions, members of trade or professional associations, customers of a single business, lodges and social clubs).

The overall objectives in the mass merchandising scheme are:

i) to obtain a high percentage of individual enrolment; and,

ii) to develop acquisition costs and continuing administrative systems which enables delivery of the insurance product at a reduced rate.

This concept can be generally divided into three distinct phases,

i) acceptance by the sponsor;

ii) the initial solicitation of employees; and,

iii) the continuing enrolment for new employees.

6) *The Package Policy Approach*
The 'package policy' is one which offers a range of cover, but which still retains flexibility, giving a base insurance plus optional additions and variations within the one contract. This has greatly affected the techniques of selling insurance. The advantage of this type of policy is that any insurance product has a large expense element and the more that can be included to obtain a higher price, the lower the unit expense cost. Put another way, the higher the average premium per policy, the more expenses can be reduced.

CHAPTER TWO

THE MARKETING VERSUS THE SALES CONCEPT
IN INSURANCE

Insurance is among the most complicated and least understood of services in today's economy. This contrasts sharply with the fact that all sectors of the population, from corporate chiefs to shop-floor operatives, make use of this service in one way or another. The major factor which contributes to this misunderstanding is the highly-complicated nature of the insurance policy itself. Individual policy holders remain confused by the small print contained in policy documents and rely on the insurance representatives to translate these terms into everyday language.

However, *some* insurance sales representatives and agents seek to capitalise on this ignorance. Through a combination of high-pressure selling techniques, they seek to mislead clients into purchasing insurance policies which they do not understand, do not need and cannot afford. Such practices, although boosting sales in the short-run, will not guarantee long-term prosperity for these companies or their agents. Existing clients will realise they have been misled and eventually no one will trust them. This practice of selling insurance through hard-driving sales techniques, where customer satisfaction is considered secondary to getting the sale, typifies what Kotler refers to as the "selling or sales concept"[11]. This philosophy rests on the assumption that customers will not buy goods or services, unless the seller makes a substantial effort to stimulate their interest in his products. The selling concept focuses attention on the adoption of sales stimulating techniques as a means of inducing customers to buy. In its extreme form, it emphasises the making of the sale, regardless of whether or not this leads to customer satisfaction. Embodied in the sales concept is the priority of satisfying the need of the seller to convert his product into cash, whereas satisfying the needs of the customer is only of peripheral consideration. Such a practice, however, is doomed in the long run, since dissatisfied customers will in future look elsewhere for products which meet their needs. According to Kotler, *"this practice will spoil the market for the seller in that eventually there will be no customers who trust him"*[11].

Insurance companies who foster the sales approach among their representatives and agents affect negatively their own long-term performance. However, it is not only their own performance and reputation which suffer, but also that of the industry as a whole, which includes the marketing orientated insurance companies as well.

9

If market orientated companies suffer as a result of the sales orientation operations of a minority of companies and their agents, they are, however, by no means the major victims. The major victims of sales orientation are, of course, the clients.

There are, therefore, three major deficiencies resulting from the adoption by insurance companies and their agents of the sales concept in its extreme hard-driving form. Firstly, it creates, at best, dissatisfaction and, at worst, suffering for clients. Secondly, it damages the reputation of the other companies in the insurance industry. Thirdly, it threatens the long-term survival of those companies which employ such techniques.

What, then, is the answer if these three problems are to be avoided? How should the sales orientated insurance companies and their agents adapt their operations in order to create satisfied customers, improve the reputation of the insurance industry and ensure their own long-term survival and prosperity?

The answer is clear — they should abandon their total reliance on the sales concept as a means of furthering their business and, in its place, should adopt a marketing approach.

Whereas the selling concept focuses attention on the need of the supplier to sell his products and convert them into cash and considers the satisfaction of the customer to be secondary, the marketing concept focuses primary attention on the needs and wants of customers and channels the efforts of the supplier towards satisfying these needs and wants. Whereas the selling concept concerns itself with the promotion of existing products to stimulate a high volume of sales, the marketing concept identifies the needs of the market and achieves sales by developing new products to satisfy these needs. While the sales concept results in profits through a high volume of sales, the marketing concept derives profits by creating and maintaining customer satisfaction. Thus, whereas the selling concept focuses on the product and how to sell it, as a means of furthering the supplier's business, the marketing concept focuses on customer needs and how to satisfy them as a means of ensuring continued prosperity to both sides: the customer and the supplier of insurance.

When applied to the insurance industry, and particularly to the sales orientated insurance companies and their agents, the marketing concept is straightforward. Instead of simply hard-selling existing and potentially unsuitable policies to unsuspecting and unwilling clients, the insurance companies should adopt the following simplified approach:

i) identify the insurance needs and wants of the market;

ii) develop appropriate insurance policies to meet these needs;

iii) determine the premium for these policies;

iv) advertise and promote these policies to potential customers;

v) organise suitable channels through which the policies are distributed to the customers; and,

vi) research and forecast future market needs (figure 2).

Figure 2
The Marketing Approach System

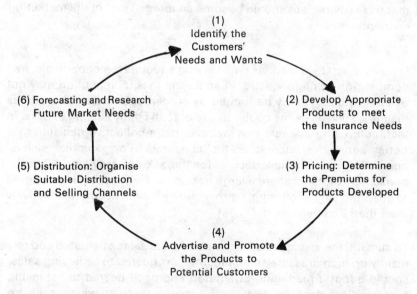

This is indeed a closed-loop system approach and the insurance company that is seriously engaged in this self-perpetuating process or marketing approach is more able to meet the competition and more efficient in doing so.

However, the role of marketing in insurance goes beyond the marketing concept definition in relation to manufactured goods and products (i.e. that of interpretation of consumers' needs and wants and the supply of the services which will produce satisfaction). Insurance organisations attempt also to produce change in the behaviour and habits of individuals in society, or in the environment of such individuals or institutions. Change, therefore, is an integral part of marketing the insurance product to individuals or social entities, in order to produce compatibility with the interests of target markets or of society as a whole. In fact, because of the quasi-collective nature of the insurance product, reflected on it by the source of the need for insurance, insurers may lobby the Government in order to produce change through laws and regulations.

Indeed, an important characteristic of the insurance product is that it has a spill-over effect, requiring that the public welfare should be taken into consideration when providing the product to the customer and that this requirement should become an integral part of the marketing concept.

Insurers operate in markets with varying structures: monopolistic, free competition or oligopolistic. In some markets, competition may not exist. In others, it may be limited by agreements among the various insurers, such as by the common use of tariffs or by sharing of risks. In fact, competing insurers may believe that a collective decision may better serve the interest of the consumer. For example, several competing insurers may decide, for the sake of providing what the consumer wants, to share a large risk. In such a case, each may agree to provide a similar offering, neither more efficient nor more effectively than their competitors.

To sum up, the insurance companies who are sales orientated and rely mainly on high pressure selling techniques geared to achieving sales, should adopt a marketing-orientated approach geared to achieving customer satisfaction. The ideal process through which such an approach can be conducted is known as the insurance marketing programme. This consists of five successive stages or elements, which are:

 i) marketing research;

 ii) product development;

iii) pricing;

iv) advertising and promotion; and,

v) distribution.

The final four elements of the insurance marketing programme comprise what is known as the *Insurance Marketing Mix*.

CHAPTER THREE

DEVELOPING THE INSURANCE MARKETING PROGRAMME

The insurance marketing programme is composed of the following five elements or steps (figure 3):

1) *Market Research* – to identify the needs and wants of the market.

2) *Product Development* – to develop insurance policies which will meet the needs of the market.

3) *Pricing* – to determine the level of the premium for these policies and how it should be paid.

4) *Advertising and Promotion* – to create widespread awareness and understanding of what the policies offer.

5) *Distribution* – the selection of suitable channels through which to distribute the policies to the customer and sales management.

The final four elements of the insurance marketing programme – product development; pricing; advertising and promotion and distribution – together comprise the Insurance Marketing Mix, or the 4 P's (product, price, promotion, place) of Insurance. It would, however, be unsatisfactory to attempt to examine the insurance marketing mix in isolation. The insurance marketing mix forms an integral part of the insurance marketing programme and any meaningful analysis of the marketing mix can only be conducted within the framework of this broader marketing approach.

The first and most basic decision underlying the development of a company's marketing programme is the type of market to be sought. For instance, a company can restrict its marketing to selected geographical areas or it can be nationwide. It can then decide on whether to concentrate on a rural or an urban operation.

To find out what the needs and wants of the customers are, extensive market research is carried out. Separate research can be done, for example, on the three major income groups – low, middle and high – so that the eventual policy will suit the customer in a particular income bracket.

Once the target market has been determined, product (policy) planning has to be carried out to determine which line the company will offer in terms of special policy features (e.g. redeemability). Then

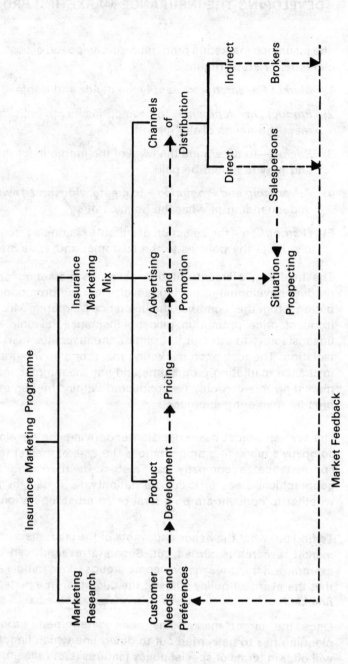

Figure 3
The Insurance Marketing Programme

the prices or premiums of each policy have to be calculated. A major element that aids in product planning and development is functional costing[12], whereby the definite costs of operation from the planning stage to the sale of the policy are determined.

After making decisions regarding market and product (i.e. insurance policy to be offered), the channels of distribution have to be considered (e.g. using a direct sales force or intermediaries). Promotional and advertising activities will also have to be introduced to support sales.

There is also the question of the magnitude of the company's sales organisation to be considered. If the company wants to maintain its position in the market or intends to increase its market share, then it will have to develop and maintain programmes for horizontal expansion of its sales force and distribution outlets.

The environment for insurance marketing is constantly changing because, for example, of rising standards of living. Although these changes are felt slowly, they must be anticipated as early as possible to cope with the challenges of ever-changing marketing conditions.

For the marketing programme to be useful, control must be enforced on the development and sales of policies. Feedback from the sales force is also essential.

Market Segmentation and Customer Behaviour

The market for insurance is not homogeneous. Like other markets, it can be segmented and, over recent years, marketing divisions of insurance companies have tried to identify different market segments and new areas of demand so that policies can be designed to suit these homogenic groups of customers (segments). For example, the life assurance market can basically be divided into two major segments – ordinary life and industrial life assurance market. However, it should be emphasised that this socio-economic distinction is only one of several which attempt to segment an aggregate life assurance market into parts characterised by different demands, requirements or needs.

The decline of industrial life assurance is one useful example of the change in the nature of life assurance products and the change in the pattern of consumer needs[13]. Possibly, the clearest segmentation by life offices has been the way they have distinguished and marketed group life assurance and personal pension bonuses. To cater for this market, some life assurance companies have established subsidiary companies that are especially designed to promote group pension and life assurance business and exploit the demand from company employees and trade unions. Besides selling these policies, the life companies, and particularly insurance brokers, also act as advisers informing their clients on the best arrangements for their group life assurance and pension schemes. Life offices have also been aware of other types of segmentation. For decades they have been aware that personal life assurance is bought for a variety of reasons which include family protection, retirement income, mortgages repayment and children's education.

Clearly, demographic influences such as age, sex, income level, occupation and geographic location have been important market determinants, but the purpose of insurance marketing requires us to consider other factors like the different types of social groups which are then further subdivided demographically. These are:

 i) weekly waged earners;

 ii) salaried employees;

 iii) self employed; and,

 iv) single women.

However, before insurance policies can be sold, additional information is necessary. It is here that the needs of the consumers play an important role — policies must be tailored to meet the consumer's requirements rather than consumers being found to buy the products.

In other areas, insurance companies have to identify and exploit new market segments. For example, unit-linked policies have laid stress on the investment aspects of life assurance marketing. The single premium bond also reached a new segment of the market, offering consumers an attractive investment alternative to building societies or to direct investment in gilts or equities. An important segment of this market that has a high potential for the marketing of life assurance is that of young married couples. Often, the first and most important purchases of life assurance are made at this stage of the life cycle. It has been found that life assurance purchases made at this time may have a lasting influence on future insurance purchases. Therefore, in order that the insurance purchasing behaviour of this particular market segment can be understood, the insurance companies should put more effort into marketing research in this area. Studies made by

Anderson and Nevin[14] have shown that the main determinants of life assurance purchasing behaviour in this particular segment were the amount of education the husband received, the amount of current and expected household income and whether any policy was purchased by either the husband or the wife. This study's findings about the U.S.A. market indicate that a less-educated husband tended to purchase more life assurance and households with either low or high income are also potential purchasers. In addition, if the husband does not possess any life policy before marriage, there is a tendency for him to purchase one after getting married and the wife plays a role in this transaction only when she actually had a policy before marriage.

Most of the insurance companies are making use of a mixture of promotion, price, distribution and product policies in order to maintain (or to increase) their share in the financial service market. However, these four groups of marketing tools are employed interactively, in what is being called "The Marketing Mix". The marketing methods used by the insurance companies have a significant effect on both the volume and types of business written. These will be considered under the headings of product (service) development, pricing, advertising and promotion and distribution (figure 4).

Behaviour characteristics are vital to understanding the insurance customer. These behavioural characteristics are basically influenced by two sets of factors:

i) *External* factors arising from influential persons and reference groups. There are two types of reference groups: membership and non-membership. Membership groups are the various groups to which the individual belongs. These include occupation, age, social class, geographic and so on. Non-membership groups are reference groups which the individual admires or aspires to belong to.

ii) *Internal* factors arise from the internal attributes of an individual. These have been identified as motives, attitudes, learned behaviour and perception. They differ from individual to individual insurance customer, according to his/her cultural and social background.

The customer's demand for insurance arises from the satisfaction which the insured gains from the increase in financial security achieved through the transfer of risk to an insurer. When considering whether to buy a policy, the customer will consider the various

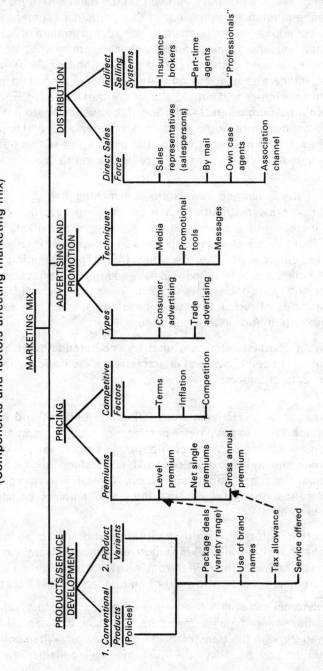

Figure 4
The Insurance Marketing Mix
(Components and factors affecting marketing mix)

alternatives open to him, taking into consideration the probability of occurence of the various hazards and their costs. It is thought that both the *size of the loss* and the *frequency of occurrence* are important. Obviously, customers differ in their attitudes to risk, security and expectancy of hazard occurrence.

Customers' preferences of one policy rather than another can be investigated by using Fishbein's formula of brand preference standing:

$$P_{pc} = \sum_{i=1}^{n} V_{ic}A_{ip}$$

where:

P_{pc} = preference standing for policy p by customer c

$i = 1, 2, 3, \ldots n$

$(0 \leqslant P_{pc} \leqslant 1)$

V_{ic} = value (i.e. relative importance) of policy attribute i to customer c

$(0 \leqslant V_{ic} \leqslant 1)$

A_{ip} = amount of attribute i believed to be possessed by policy (brand) p

$(0 < A_{ip} \leqslant 1)$

Using the equation above, preferences for the various insurance policies offered on the market can be calculated and the market researcher might be able to suggest which is the most preferred policy (among alternative ones), which is the second best and so on. Obviously, preference standing will differ from one customer segment to another. The first problem is to identify the attributes that are considered of importance (or related) to a certain insurance product (see table 2 column 1). This can be done through in-depth interviews with actual or potential buyers of certain types of insurance products. Then, through interviews or questionnaires and data collection, the relative importance of attributes (i's) for the representative sample of customers interviewed *and* the amount of attribute (i) believed to be part of the various insurance policies offered can be obtained.

Table 2
Life Insurance Segmentation
Characteristics, Reasons for Buying and Bases for Segmentation

(1) Differential Characteristics	(2) Reasons for Buying	(3) Main Bases for Segmentation
1. Premium size	a) Family protection	i) Demographic, e.g.: age sex income level geographical location
2. Frequency of payment	b) Provision for old age	
3. Policy redeemability	c) Mortgage repayment	
4. Risk of default (as assessed by insured)	d) Payment of education fees	ii) Social groups, e.g.: wage earners self employed women students
5. Agent/agency service	e) Saving for emergencies	

Insurance buying behaviour can be systematically analysed in five stages as follows:

Figure 5
Insurance Buying Behaviour

1. Decide on the "best" type of insurance.

    ↓

2. Estimate the amount of insurance required.

    ↓

3. Consider the factors that are important in selecting a certain insurer.

    ↓

4. Evaluate the various insurers on each of the factors (attributes) identified (in stage 3).

    ↓

5. Buy a certain policy.

1. Decide on the best type of insurance — on the type of policy that suits the customer's needs and wants (e.g. endowment life insurance or ordinary life assurance).

2. Estimate amount of insurance required. In making a rational decision the potential customer should forecast future risks and hazards on one hand and estimate future incomes and financial needs on the other.

3. There are a number of factors that might be important in selecting a certain insurer (e.g. agent's personality and friendliness, agent's professional capability, insurance premiums and terms and insurer's reputation).

4. Each of the attributes above (for a more comprehensive list see Table 3) are evaluated by the customer and then a decision is made.

Studies have been undertaken in the U.S.A. to establish customers' attitudes towards insurance[15]. The most important reasons for selecting a certain company were:

i) its reputation/reliability (60%);

ii) quality of the policy (26%); and,

iii) policy benefits (14%).

23

Consumer expectations from an insurance policy usually extend beyond the promises made by the company in its contract. The insurance buyer views the product not just as a contract or policy offering certain coverage(s) but – depending on his perceptions, personality, cultural and social environment – as a package of services designed "to solve" certain problems.

Indeed, customers believe that the insurance service extends beyond contract agreements. For example, in property and liability insurance the policy stipulates certain "contract services" (e.g. liability coverage, repair or replacement of property). However, there are additional services that the insurance customer *expects* from the insurance company outside the policy agreement. These non-contract (or temporal) services can be classified as follows:[16]

i) *Services to be provided before the sale* – advice to the potential customer on risk analysis, policy planning and a general interest in his welfare.

ii) *Services during the period of the policy* – risk re-appraisal (i.e. re-evaluation of insurance needs), policy renewal dates and up-to-date information.

iii) *Services at the time of claims* – filling out claim forms.

Overall consumer buying behaviour is dependent upon a number of variables, the most important ones being his/her:

a) attitudes toward risk; and,

b) socio-economic characteristics.

CHAPTER FOUR

TYPES OF MARKET SEGMENTATION

Segmentation involves identifying customer groups which are fairly homogeneous in themselves, but which are different from other customer types. Its purpose is to determine differences between customers which are of relevance to the marketing decision maker. Obviously, the person in the street requiring a small household insurance policy, for example, will require a different approach to that of, say, a business wishing to insure its capital equipment for a large sum. Still further segmentation is possible: private individual behaviour will be affected by social class, age, sex, income group or geographic location, as elaborated below. The more characteristics the market is segmented by, the more precise is the insurer's knowledge of his customer.

The questions employed in the insurance market research tests ask six basic questions:

i) who is the customer;

ii) what does the market buy;

iii) when does the market buy;

iv) who is involved in the buying;

v) why does the customer buy; and,

vi) how does the insured buy?

The information gained has been used to improve the design of insurance products and communications with insurance customers. Many of the current insurance marketing efforts concentrate on segmenting the market into customer groups with different needs, buying styles and responses to promotions. Strategies are then developed to appeal to the identified segments.

Many insurers have for years designed their promotional and marketing efforts to aim at only the very broad mass markets. Their philosophy has been to utilise a "shotgun" or "blanket" approach, in the hope that something in their advertising message would strike a responsive cord with someone. In most instances, insurance companies were not sure who that someone might be. The term "mass market" suggests a homogeneity of needs on the part of the customer. Recently, however, insurers have become increasingly aware of the possible improvements in productivity and resulting economies to scale by using market segmentation, when appealing to new customers or promoting insurance services to present customers.

In order to gain a full appreciation of the way in which market segmentation can benefit the insurance industry, it is first necessary to understand the concept itself. Market segmentation has been defined as a means of guiding marketing strategy by distinguishing customer groups and needs. Segmentation is the subdividing of a market into distinct subsets of customers, where any subset may conceivably be selected as a market target to be reached with a distinct marketing mix. In essence, the key to market segmentation is to take the so-called mass market, with a heterogeneous set of needs and, through the use of creative research efforts, divide it up into smaller parts or segments, each reflecting a homogeneous set of needs, thus giving the insurance marketer some direction in shaping his product offerings. The major benefit that will accrue to the insurance company is that it may be able to promote more effectively to each of the smaller relatively homogeneous markets than could be done to the larger heterogeneous market.

There are three conditions that must be met for effective segmentation. First, the characteristics of a segment must be identifiable and measurable. Second, it should be accessible in that it must be possible to reach a segment effectively with proper marketing strategies. Third, a segment must have the potential to generate profit. A fourth criterion for market segmentation that may be added is that each segment should react uniquely to different marketing efforts. The reason why different market segments exist and why there is a need to treat them separately, stems from one of the most fundamental aspects of marketing — the customer buying process.

The process itself is simple in concept. First the person experiences a need which he wants to satisfy. This "need arousal" can be due to certain perceptions and attitudes towards risk, the life style of the individual or the promotional activity of an insurer. Once the person is aware of this need, he then sets about determining the alternative ways by which it can be satisfied. He or she does this by evaluating each alternative against the other alternatives, using his own criterion as individually perceived and weighted by him and selecting the alternative that best meets his requirements. A typical example in the case of insurance would be the person who is dis-satisfied with the service which he is receiving from his present insurer and wishes to find an alternative one that offers a better service. He would obtain information about each of the insurance companies available and their services and products and, using that information which he considers reliable (irrespective of its actual accuracy and completeness), he will evaluate each insurer against the others in terms of whatever criteria he considers important. There are three major types of insurance market segmentation:

  i) segmentation by life cycle;

  ii) psychographic segmentation; and,

  iii) social classes segmentation.

In addition, there is an interest now in identifying special insurance consumers (e.g. students and working women) and offering "special" products to these segments.

1) *Segmentation by Life Cycle*

Hass and Berry[17] advocate the classification of financial customers in households according to their stages in the life cycle. There is ample evidence, according to them, that the financial needs and expectations of households will vary according to their stages in the life cycle. For example, although young married couples with no children have the same size household as older couples whose children no longer live at home, the insurance needs of these two segments, which an insurance marketer should identify, would tend to differ in certain respects.

The life cycle segments are:

  i) the bachelor stage – young single people;

  ii) newly-married couples – young, no children;

  iii) the full nest I – young married couples with dependent children;

  iv) the full nest II – older married couples with dependent children;

  v) the empty nest – older married couples with no children living with them; and,

  vi) the solitary survivors – older single people.

Segmentation by life cycle provides a good starting point for an effective packaging or systematisation of insurance products.

2) Psychographic Segmentation

Psychographic segmentation utilises consumer life styles and person-ality differences to determine variances in buyer demands. For example, the insurance companies market differently to swingers (young, unmarried, active, fun-loving, party-going people, seeking up-to-date goods and fast-paced hedonistic living), than to "plain Joes" (older, married, home-centred, family-centred people seeking ordinary, unfrilled goods that do their job). Indeed, insurance companies price differently life policies which are designed for smokers or motor policies for fast sports car drivers.

Psychographic segmentation has its uses in selling insurance. For example, an insurance salesperson might discover that independent, relatively aggressive entrepreneurs respond to a personal selling approach characterised by passive, unstructured advice-giving, whereas the more dependent (the less aggressive) middle management of commercial insured large corporations respond better to a more structured, authoritative sales presentation.

Psychographic segmentation is useful for:[18]

i) *Predicting behaviour.* By identifying a customer segment and understanding why its members are interested in making an insurance related decision, it is possible to estimate the probability that they will react in a certain way, or at least predict several possible reactions.

ii) *Client interaction.* The process of psychographic segmentation allows more effective communication between a customer and the insurer, as a more meaningful dialogue, with more information, will flow both ways.

iii) *Anticipation of future market needs.* With valuable information flowing in from customers, it will provide a better opportunity to analyse future customer requirements. It will also help to provide a basis for determining future insurance objectives.

iv) *Relevance of practice.* By understanding the behavioural patterns of customers, insurance services can be tailored to meet changing customer needs and demands. The idea is to meet as many of the needs of a target market as possible.

3) Social Classes Segmentation

Insurers traditionally used purely demographic information to analyse their customers and, initially, segmentation in insurance was basically along demographic lines. Categories such as age, sex, education, income, family size and religion were used. Such terms as "house-wives", "consumers", "men", "women", "buyers", "investors" or "savers" were used casually. However, it was soon realised that this form of segmentation was very general and was often used as a matter of convenience.

There are basically two approaches to the so-called segmentation by social class:

i) *Geographic segmentation* examines potential differences in the relative attractiveness of different marketing mixes by geographical location of the consumer's home, or of a company's plant facilities and offices.

ii) *Demographic segmentation* occurs when the insurance marketer determines that customers respond differently to marketing offerings on the basis of their age, sex, size of immediate family, income level, occupation, formal education, religion, race or stage in the family life cycle. Demographics are a popular basis for segmentation since they often have a strong and significant relationship to an insurer's sales and are easier to recognise and measure than most other variables.

4) *Other Consumer Segments*
This section focuses on segments which have already been briefly mentioned, but which deserve special attention.

i) *Women.* With the liberation of women and the trend towards equal opportunities, women are increasingly featured and take a growing role in the economy. Bearing in mind that they form something like 50% of the population, they demand very special attention on the very basis of substantiality. For the insurance sector, the new independent role of women means a new market segment, whether they are single, married or unmarried mothers.

Previously, insurance companies have neglected this market and have even been accused of treating women as second class citizens in terms of services offered. Lately, insurers have come to terms with the new situation and have adopted special measures to tap the women's market. Primarily, they have recognised that an increasing number of women are attaining management positions through better education opportunities and, as such, are capable of exerting commercial influence. In addition, the financial independence of women means that insurance companies can assume a special role in maintaining independence and security.

29

In September, 1974, Langham Life Assurance in the U.K. launched the first insurance plan for women. Its objective was to *"enable women to enjoy a greater measure of financial self-sufficiency throughout life and retirement"*, (*Policy-Holder*, September, 1974). The objective of this launch was to provide a policy where women's special needs were recognised (e.g. the life assurance policy *included*, for the first time, disabilities caused by pregnancy or childbirth as an acceptable clause).

In addition, women's role in the insurance industry is emphasised by the fact that over 80% of all the insurance agents in the U.S.A. are female and in Japan, for example, women are particularly preferred for selling insurance.

ii) *Students.* Various references have been made to this segment in this book. Here the picture as a whole is presented in an attempt to integrate the information available. This segment has been recognised recently by insurers for its future potential and measures aimed to cater especially for students are based on the philosophy that students will retain their loyalty (after graduation), unless they have a major reason to do otherwise. On the other hand, the student market segment is considered to carry quite high risks by the insurance industry, particularly because of students' high incidence of loss of personal belongings and proneness to car or motor cycle accidents.

Despite this the student market has recently received increasing interest because of the untapped size of this segment. There are insurance brokers which specialise in this segment (e.g. Endsleigh in London), although more recently certain banks (e.g. Barclays) have come forward with competitive student cover packages.

Very recently, Norwich Union has started an aggressive advertising and promotional campaign aimed at the student market. Promotional material and applications for insurance cover (particularly for students' personal property during the term time) are offered to students at the reduced price of £9.50 per cover (1983/84 academic year) through the various departments at Universities and Polytechnics. Harrisons (Norwich Union) of Oxford offers advice to students on buying life cover. They suggest that a short-term contract is more useful and cheaper to students. In addition, Harrisons are now giving grants of £50 to £180 to help with the early years' premiums for students and graduates without jobs who are still interested in *long-term* life cover.

CHAPTER FIVE

MARKETING RESEARCH

The development of marketing research in the insurance industry has resulted from the growth of marketing management and the marketing concept. The basic purpose of applying marketing research methods in insurance is to reduce marketing management risks and consequently embrace higher marketing efficiency. The need for marketing research in insurance exists particularly when:

i) there is a high degree of marketing uncertainty or disagreement amongst the marketing executives about the 'right' marketing decision; and/or,

ii) some type of marketing research technique is available and its employment will increase the amount and/or reliability of information on the basis of which a marketing decision can be made.

Objectives

Basic marketing research studies in insurance focus on the customers, their profiles, preferences, tendencies and habits, etc. Marketing research studies attempt to investigate a variety of problems.

1) *Revenue and profit potentials from selling additional/certain insurance products to various insurance customers segments*

This is important since identification and targeting of important customer segments might call for significant changes in the marketing strategy (i.e. the allocation of marketing resources). Given systematic profit measures, insurance marketing management might be able to predict systematically the profitability of obtaining a given number of additional customers, measuring at the same time the cost of obtaining these customers through various alternative marketing methods (e.g. advertising and/or promotion and/or price discounts and/or "new" distribution channels and/or 'new'/modified insurance products).

2) *Customer-prospect profile studies, industry shopping or distribution studies*

These study the effectiveness of salespersons in presenting and selling insurance.

3) *Concept test new insurance services or new packages to be offered*

A concept test will, for example, deal with the problem of how to market a new package offered to several different market segments and which market strategy should be adopted for each segment. This will enable the company to select the optimum marketing strategy and to increase the chances of success for the planned insurance product. In the health insurance field in the U.S.A., this technique has been used to measure the appeal of alternative special insurance features such as psychiatric services, dental care or in-home nursing care[19]. The information obtained from such a study might enable the insurance company to make feasible decisions in relation to the price (premium) the policy is to be offered at, what should be the insurance product characteristics and how it should be advertised (what media, what kind of message, how frequent and at what times, etc.).

4) *Systematic continuous studies particularly on customers' intentions*

An insurance company in the U.S.A. used to conduct annual studies which measured, among other things, shopping intentions the next time people had to renew their automobile insurance[19]. The advertising goal of this company was to encourage prospects to shop or price the company's insurance which was cheaper than several other competitors. Customers' shopping intentions studies might indeed enable more efficient marketing resources allocation. Continuous systematic studies may enable the insurance company to predict their near future market share, attitudes towards the company's attributes and services and the awareness level towards the company's products.

5) *Effectiveness research*

Optimisation of marketing resources allocation requires a number of studies. Research on advertising effectiveness can contribute to better spending levels, optimal advertising themes and improving the definition of the advertising market target. For example, a major insurance company has moved its advertisements from general purpose magazines to specialised sports journals, because it discovered that its customers' characteristics were met more by these sports journals. It is, however, extremely important to study and consider carefully the cost of generating additional insurance sales from different customer segments through advertising, in order to be able to make rational advertising and sales efforts decisions.

Particular questions that can be answered by a market research study for an insurance company are:

i) At what age does a chance of selling a certain type of insurance policy maximise?

ii) What criteria/factors lead to an increase in the interest/willingness to purchase an insurance product?

iii) What are the roles of the marketing mix elements (personal selling, advertising, variety of products offered, merchandising and pricing) in creating an insurance policy purchase?

iv) Why do certain customers buy from competitors and how should a company change its image in order to create a sale?

v) What are the perceived advantages and limitations of competitive insurance companies in relation to a particular insurance company and how important are each of these advantages and limitations? What are the correlations between the various pairs of variables (advantages, limitations, constraints)? Can they be generalised (factor analysed) for effective marketing conclusions, decisions and actions?

Marketing Research Experiments

Marketing research information can be obtained through questionnaires, attitude scaling techniques, marketing experimentations, observations and simulations. There are very few, if any, marketing simulation studies in insurance. Most of the research data is collected through questionnaires which make extensive use of attitude scaling and marketing experimentations. There are three major types of possible marketing experimentation in insurance:

i) direct sales experiments;

ii) geographical experimentation; and,

iii) direct mail,

the first two being particularly popular and applicable in insurance.

33

i) *Direct sales experiments* can be employed by insurance companies who use direct distribution channels extensively. These experiments enable the company to test alternative selling approaches by selecting samples of insurance salespersons and providing them with specific marketing mix strategies. This kind of testing will provide information on the profitability of certain market segments, the effectiveness of various marketing mix strategies and the potential of new insurance products and their characteristics.

ii) *Geographical experimentation* is undertaken when separate insurance marketing efforts on chosen geographical area(s) are feasible. For example, before a new insurance product is launched nationally, the product is offered initially – and for a certain period only – using a certain mix of marketing techniques in a particular area/territory. This approach might enable the insurance marketing department to decide on the most suitable marketing strategy *before* the insurance product is launched nationally, thereby improving its chances of success.

iii) *Direct mail* experimentations involve sending direct mail information (e.g. on new insurance products or new advertising themes on old products) to certain selected groups of customers. By tracing the level of sales to each of these groups, it might be possible to determine the best alternative product or the most effective advertising message and to predict the revenues produced by these alternatives.

The marketing data collected by whatever method of data collection selected should then be analysed through a univariate or, more usually, multivariate methods[20]. The results ought to be 'interpreted' and 'translated' into marketing recommendations for action. Most of the standard marketing research approaches, methods and techniques are also suitable for analysing marketing situations in insurance companies. The best general and basic marketing research texts that can be used for marketing research formulations are Kinnear and Taylor[21] and/or Fitzroy[22]. The major difference between these two textbooks is that while the first is method orientated, the second is problem orientated. However, both these texts – as well as many others – deal mainly with examples of products (rather than services) in marketing research situations.

Investigating Insurance Selection Criteria

A marketing research study on a specific market segment— the *student market* — to ascertain insurance selection criteria has been performed recently by the author. The U.K. student population is around one million and, because of recent increased competition amongst the insurance companies, there is a growing interest in the potential of the student insurance market. The student insurance market, like almost any other sizeable population, can be segmented by sex, age, life styles, economic and social background, home and overseas students and past experience with insurance services, etc. The basic objective of this market research study was to segment the student population in order to identify, quantify and analyse the correlations amongst the variables that influence the choice of an insurance policy by these particular customers.

From in-depth interviews with marketing executives in various insurance companies, discussions with a small sample of university and colleges students and review of published literature[23] on the subject, 18 major variables that affect this segment's choice of an insurance policy have been identified (Table 3). A questionnaire asking the respondents to identify the level of importance they attach to each of the 18 variables on a 7 points scale (from 1: "Not important at all" to 7: "Extremely important") was employed. In total 370 students at four universities and four polytechnics completed these questionnaires through personal interviews. The questionnaires also provided information on whether the respondents were home or overseas students, insured or uninsured, undergraduate or postgraduate and, if insured, what kind of policy held (life/car insurance/travel insurance/some other policy).

Table 3
The Variables Affecting Insurance Selection Criteria

1. Reputation of the insurance company.

2. Variety of policies offered.

3. Flexibility of policies (i.e. special terms and conditions adjusted to individual needs and requirements can be arranged).

4. Size of premium (price).

5. Surrender value of policy (i.e. the lump sum payment and bonus to be received when policy expires).

6. Promptness of service.

7. Advice and help.

8. Friendliness of insurance agent.

9. Availability (i.e. number of branches and agencies).

10. Profitability of policy.

11. Policy time horizon (i.e. when the savings/profit can be cashed).

12. Provisions for inflation (i.e. adjustment of premiums to take care of inflation).

13. Rate of tax allowances.

14. Financial facilities offered by insurance company.

15. Package deal.

16. Gifts premium.

17. Insurance company advertising campaign.

18. Reimbursement after policy cancellation.

The size of the four segments of student population that emerged were:

	Number	Percentage (%)
Non insured	162	44
Insured	208	56
Overseas students	74	20
Home students	296	80
Total population	370	100

As the data investigated was attitudinal (i.e. ordinal scaled), non-metric statical measures (the Spearman rank-order correlation coefficient and profile analysis) were employed in this study. The correlation analysis for the home students segment (significant at 0.01 level) is presented in table 4 and the profile analysis of the insured vs uninsured students for the total sample of 370 students is presented in figure 6.

In interpreting the correlation coefficients, the following arbitrary scale was used:

1 r_s n less than 0.10   =   negligible correlation
2 r_s of 0.11 to 0.30   =   weak correlation
3 r_s of 0.31 to 0.49   =   fair correlation
4 r_s of 0.50 to 0.69   =   strong correlation
5 r_s of 0.70 to 0.89   =   very strong correlation
6 r_s of 0.90 or higher were considered to indicate perfect correlation

Table 4
Non-parametric (Spearman) Correlation Coefficients of Attitudes on Insurance Selection

(Home students only; n = 296; significance = 0.01)

Variables affecting insurance selection	1	2	3	4	5	6	7	8	9	10	11	12	13	14	15	16	17	18
1. Representing the insurance company	–																	
2. Variety of policies offered	.38	–																
3. Flexibility of policies offered	.31	.46	–															
4. Size of premium (price)	.03	.11	.03	–														
5. Surrender value of policy	.22	.23	.19	.19	–													
6. Promptness of service	.15	.21	.24	.03	.13	–												
7. Advice and help	.21	.31	.42	–.10	.13	.46	–											
8. Friendliness of insurance agent	.11	.26	.19	–.04	.11	.33	.42	–										
9. Availability (i.e. number of branches and agencies)	.23	.27	.20	.05	.19	.28	.33	.29	–									
10. Profitability of the policy	.14	.27	.15	.07	.38	.16	.10	.36	–.01	–								
11. Policy time horizon (when savings/profits can be cashed)	.13	.24	.20	.13	.33	.23	.22	.11	.11	.53	–							
12. Provisions for inflation	.19	.20	.25	.10	.27	.11	.29	.04	.10	.41	.42	–						
13. Rate of tax allowance	.14	.21	.22	–.02	.27	.29	.29	.04	.15	.38	.36	.52	–					
14. Financial facilities offered by the insurance company	.24	.24	.23	–.05	.24	.17	.29	.18	.30	.17	.34	.52	.30	–				
15. Package deal	.23	.33	.30	.12	.19	.17	.18	.28	.19	.20	.26	.25	.33	.40	–			
16. Gifts premium	.14	.20	.20	.02	.21	.18	.23	.23	.30	.35	.16	.34	.28	.42	.45	–		
17. Insurance Company advertising campaign	.05	.03	–.08	.07	.05	.11	.10	.25	.31	.11	.07	.05	.03	.17	.22	.39	–	
18. Reimbursement after policy cancellation	.12	.09	.26	.06	.33	.15	.16	.00	.09	.16	.32	.31	.40	.34	.27	.21	.05	–

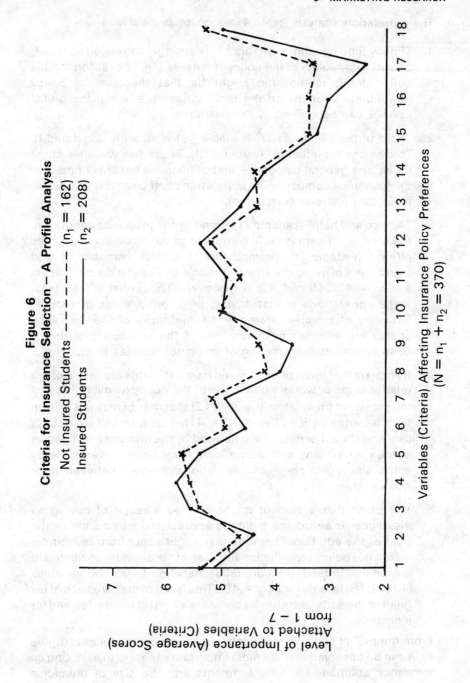

Figure 6
Criteria for Insurance Selection – A Profile Analysis

Not Insured Students ------ ($n_1 = 162$)
Insured Students ———— ($n_2 = 208$)

Variables (Criteria) Affecting Insurance Policy Preferences
($N = n_1 + n_2 = 370$)

Level of Importance (Average Scores)
Attached to Variables (Criteria)
from 1 – 7

The correlation analysis (table 4) suggests as follows:

1. "Policy time horizon" (variable 11) is strongly correlated ($r_s = .53$) to the "profitability of the policy" (variable 10). The reason for this quite strong relationship might be that the level of policy profitability depends on the time horizon (i.e. when the profit/ savings can be cashed by the customer).

2. "Rate of tax allowance(s)" (variable 13) is strongly correlated to "provisions for inflation" (variable 12). These two variables come under one general category – that of financial benefits offered by the insurance company. The correlation coefficient is $r_s = .52$, (i.e. indicating a strong correlation).

3. "Advice and help" (variable 7) offered by the insurance agents (i.e. the service offered) is fairly correlated to the flexibility of policies offered (variable 3), promptness of service (variable 6) and friendliness of insurance agents (variable 8). Correlation coefficients are: $r_s = .42, .46$ and $.42$, respectively. The probable reason for these correlations is that advice, help, promptness of service, flexibility of policies offered and friendliness of the insurance agents are all different dimensions of the service factor that is quite important in marketing of insurance policies to students.

4. It appears that most of the insured home students are aware of the relationships between profitability of the policy (variable 10) and the provision for inflation (variable 12) that may or may not exist in the insurance policy offered ($r_s = .41$). This financial awareness can, and should perhaps, be employed by the insurance companies in their advertising and promotional campaigns, for example by emphasising gifts premium (correlation coefficient between these two variables is $r_s = .39$).

5. The profit that a student might gain as a result of buying an insurance or assurance policy is appreciated particularly in the light of the additional benefits that might occur from reimbursement after policy cancellation because of tax allowances related to the policy. Indeed, the correlation between these two variables (13 and 18) is fairly high ($r_s = .40$). This issue of the clawback of tax relief in the early years has a very serious impact on the demand for insurance.

From the profile analysis of the insured vs uninsured students (figure 6), it can be observed that the most important variables in selecting an insurance company for both segments are: the size of premiums (price), flexibility of policies offered and the surrender value of the policy. The major difference here is that uninsured students attach a higher importance to the reputation of the insurance company (variable 1), while the insured students attach a higher importance to provisions for inflation made in the policy offered (variable 12).

Both insured and uninsured students attach little or no importance to variables like insurance company advertising campaign, gifts premiums and package deals. There are certain differences between uninsured vs insured students' attitudes on variables influencing their selection of an insurance company. These differences can be seen in figure 6. The profile analysis has been obtained by averaging the scores of the respective student categories on each of the 18 variables.

It is easy to see why variables such as premium size, inflation provision, reimbursement, policy profitability and surrender value are important — they all represent a tangible loss or a tangible gain in financial terms to the respondent. Policy flexibility will be attractive to the students, because they all consider themselves as "special cases" and like to have insurance policies tailored to their special needs.

The findings of the profile analysis indicate how these two different market segments should be approached. Obviously the marketing effort in implementing the various market strategies should depend on the size and the growth potential of the relevant market segments. The importance of this type of market research is that it indicates segment attitudes on the various factors and variables that affect customers' behaviour. This information is of obvious importance in selecting feasible and cost efficient marketing orientated strategies for an insurance company.

CHAPTER SIX

PRODUCT DEVELOPMENT

The first step in the insurance marketing programme – identifying the needs and wants of the market – is conducted through a programme of market research. The adoption of marketing research in the insurance industry as a means of identifying the needs of the market is a relatively new phenomenon, but it is becoming increasingly important in a world of intense competition, as a method of searching out new markets.

Once marketing research is carried out to identify who the potential customers are and to determine exactly what they want, the second step in the insurance marketing programme (and the first element of the insurance marketing mix) is to create, or develop, insurance policies which will meet the needs of these customers.

Insurance products are important in determining the competitive behaviour of the insurance companies and the structure of the assurance markets. Individual insurance companies do not always serve the same market. In addition to varying philosophies about fields of operation, individual companies might vary considerably in the range and type of contracts made available. The need for product differentiation may well make it initially impossible for the average buyer to make any comparison between the contracts of two individual companies (e.g. the premium redistributions involved in modified life contracts or variations in early cash values)[24].

Similarly, package or combination policies further complicate the decision on which policy is suitable to meet the needs of an individual. The contracts of individual companies also differ with regard to 'liberality', in that settlement options included in an individual contract may be more liberal with one company than another. The guaranteed cash values may differ considerably from company to company, and even within a given company on different contracts. There is no standard insurance policy/contract except for the standard provisions as required by law. Only competition causes a tendency towards uniformity. Thus, when a new benefit or contract feature is introduced successfully by one company, others tend to adopt it too. However, competition also works against uniformity. It serves as an incentive for companies to develop distinctive and improved contract features to differentiate their products and be able to make the best competitive showing.

As real disposable income per capita has generally risen all over the world, sales of insurance policies (particularly life insurance savings) have also increased, often through the use of more sophisticated products. In recent years, insurance companies have stressed the tax advantages of certain policies (e.g. life assurance to potential home buyers). In some policies where a pension scheme is included, the assurance companies have made use of the publicity given to pensions. With the implementation of the new state pension schemes[13], companies have marketed an increasing number of these policies which allow the contributor full tax relief on the premiums paid.

Insurance policies on products can be generally categorised in two broad groups: conventional products and variant products.

Conventional Products

Conventional products can be classified into two main categories — policies which provide protection and policies which provide a mixture of protection *and* investment. These two types of major conventional products (in life assurance only) are presented below:

Figure 7
Conventional Life Assurance Products

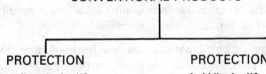

CONVENTIONAL PRODUCTS

PROTECTION
1. Non-profit whole life
2. Endowment
3. Basic term
4. Convertible term
5. Basic term & income benefit

PROTECTION/INVESTMENT
1. Whole life with profit
2. Endowment with profit

Protection policies include non-profit whole life and endowment policies. However, the simplest of all protection policies and one that is largely ignored, is term or temporary assurance, whereby the policy holder is given protection for a limited period of time (e.g. 10 to 15 years)[25]. A variation of the basic term assurance is a convertible term, whereby the policy holder is given the option to convert to another type of policy at any time during the policy term, even if his health deteriorates. Frequently, term assurances are linked to a family income benefit policy. At present, term assurance is still an under-exploited form of protection due to the lack of public awareness. One reason for this is that term assurance is seldom marketed actively, since the low premium provides low commission for brokers and does not create sufficient incentive for the salespersons whose job performances are measured primarily by premium income.

Policies which provide a mixture of protection and investment include profit-participating endowment and whole life policies. Profits from such policies come from reversionary bonuses which are added annually or biannually to the policy.

Product Variants

As part of a general attempt to remain competitive, both within the savings market and in the provision of insurance policies, insurance companies have developed a large number of product variants, each suited or designed to meet the requirements of different types of customers.

In life assurance, the original distinction between ordinary life and industrial life assurance provides another excellent example of the life companies' early awareness of the needs of different groups of customers. Similarly, the creation of whole life policies, designed to offer life assurance over the whole life of the policy holder and the creation of endowment assurance are further examples of the way in which the basic product has been varied to suit different needs.

The result of this technical differentiation is the existence of a large number of different insurance policies (products). Government restrictions on the types of insurance policies which qualify for tax relief do, however, restrain the development and diffusion of further products, although the existing range of products is likely to be enlarged and modified over the future.

Assuming insurance policies have all the listed characteristics mentioned in Table 5, then product differentiation is technically possible by varying one or more of the characteristics listed there. Where companies vary characteristics in ways not experienced before (e.g. offering guaranteed surrender values), then the introduction of such characteristics is likely to provide a major competitive advantage, at least so long as no imitations occur and provided consumers do strongly desire such characteristics.

45

Table 5
Main Properties of Insurance Products

Characteristics	Type of Product
1. Premium Payment	Single premium policy, annual, quarterly or monthly premiums. (The monthly premiums are particularly important.)
2. Redeemability	Surrender values can be an important influence on consumer choice and frequently have been incorporated into policies. This is used as a competitive weapon by some companies.
3. Term Versus Maturity	This is used to differentiate whole life policies and endowment policies from term insurance.
4. Risk	The risk of default is difficult to quantify technically. The consumer usually considers it to be associated with the company's image, reputation and size.
5. Claim Payment	Varies with the type of policy (e.g. annuities involve frequent payments, whilst others involve a single payment by the company).

Product Innovation

Although new products in the insurance industry are not subject to 'copyright' as such, they still represent an important method of stimulating the growth of the company. Due to the competitive nature of the industry, insurance innovations are adopted at a much faster rate than they were forty years ago[26]. Thus the relative advantage held by the innovating company is short-lived. The marketing strategies of these companies must also balance the benefits and costs of the new product or service offering against other marketing or cost production opportunities[27]. Insurance innovations are said to be less costly than those of tangible goods, with the main costs being attributed to actuarial time to analyse feasibility and to advertising – to attract the customers' attention. This condition arises from the fact that 'copyright' is absent from the world of insurance, so competitors are not deterred from adopting each others' ideas or insurance plans. Indeed, a major study in the U.S.A.[26] supports this claim. Of the insurance companies included in the study, 68% confirmed that they have obtained ideas for new insurance products after 'careful analysis' of their competitors' products. About half the companies investigated suggested that some form of organised procedures or programmes is needed to stimulate new product innovation in insurance.

Product innovation offers a new choice to consumers. Since no one product will be suitable for use by all types of policy holder, the introduction of a new policy will be aimed at a target market. Besides product innovation, there is another form of innovation called *process innovation* whereby there is a change in how the product is produced or marketed, making possible a lower cost and hence a lower price[28].

Product innovations can be divided into four categories:

i) <u>*Contract.*</u> The policy format and coverage are altered (e.g. family income policy).

ii) <u>*Policy provisions.*</u> There are changes in specific policy provisions including the underwriting or rating of a policy (e.g. retirement income policy).

iii) <u>*Marketing methods.*</u> Variations in the channels of distribution.

iv) <u>*Services.*</u> Establishment of new customer benefits unrelated to contractual provisions.

Competition from other forms of savings such as banks, unit trusts and index-linked schemes, have caused the insurance industry many traumas and, in the event, gave rise to the creation of unit-linked and index-linked policies specifically designed to offer policy holders a share in the profits. For example, the linked life policies were designed to capture a segment of the savings market which is characterised by the saver's wealth and income status as well as their willingness to gamble. This type of unit-linked contract also presented an opportunity for new life companies to break down the barriers of entry to an industry which would have been impenetrable to newcomers if they had tried to compete on conventional contracts.

Sources of ideas for insurance products/services development can stem from suggestions from agents or other field representatives or by analysing competitors' products. Sometimes, special innovating groups are used specifically to develop a new product. Occasionally, direct suggestions from policy holders can also give rise to product innovations.

One of the techniques used by the insurance companies include product variation in an attempt to differentiate between products offered by different companies. Product variation can be achieved by product innovation, an important strategic weapon for a company, or by modification of existing products. However, the success of these new products depends to a large extent on the company's marketing strategy. At the same time, the lack of copyright on new policies means that a new policy is not unique to a particular company for very long.

New products are being developed almost every day in an attempt to satisfy the needs of the particular society, market or segment. Amongst the relative new product innovations in insurance there are insurance against 'gazumping', dental insurance, life cycle policies (i.e. insurance products that are offered to potential customers at different stages in the life cycle), real estate investment plans, hospital and surgical insurance, medical insurance plans including preventive care, combining property with life insurance (cheaper as well), joint sales policies (i.e. individual policies to group certificate holders), legal insurance to cover medical doctors or leading solicitors from potential high legal claims (particularly in the U.S.A. these claims might be very high), inflation guard endorsement, family auto (car) policy and replacement cost coverage, etc., etc.

In certain lines of insurance, insurers provide more than an insurance cover. For example, in lines of engineering insurance, insurers provide advice, carry out inspections and recommend changes aimed at reducing risks, while in marine hull insurance, insurers provide inspection services, maritime intelligence and information. In some large insurance companies, in order to expand the service provided, risk management organisations have been established to deal with the environment of the consumer. Through risk management, insurers not only help in drawing the insurance plan, but also assist consumers in detecting areas of risk and in analysing and measuring such risks.

To sum up, the reasons for product innovation in insurance are:[15]

  i) to gain a competitive advantage;

 ii) to stimulate salespersons (particularly in the life insurance business);

iii) the result of court decisions;

iv) the result of regulation and consumer protection laws; and,

v) following the recommendation of agency departments (branches).

Developing insurance products as a result of agency (branch) recommendation is probably most effective, particularly in life assurance, as salespersons can assist here not just with the selling of the new policy, but also with product design, pricing (ratemaking) and pretesting.

There are, however, a number of obstacles to insurance product development. The greatest obstacle is regulation by a government or state authority. Insurance salespersons, customers and finding reinsurance are also obstacles to insurance product development.

As there are no patents or copyrights on most insurance products, when a new product is introduced, if it demonstrates market appeal, it is likely to be copied in a very short time. Obviously, in order to launch a new product effectively, two conditions have to be met:

i) statutory requirements; and,

ii) reinsurance.

Statutory requirements refer to the regulations in force in various countries which govern the operation of insurance companies/agencies. For example, developing new products in the life assurance business would require a certificate to start that activity or a minimum amount of capital, etc.

Reinsurance is essential in any successful insurance activity. There are two reasons for this. Firstly, insurance companies need to reinsure a certain amount of their exposure (risks), because the total risk might be too great for that particular company. In addition, insurance accounting conventions require that all expenses of writing new business are deducted from income in the year in which the policy is sold. Normally expenses plus statutory reserves required are larger than the first year premium, so reinsurance is necessary. No doubt reinsurance provides essential organisational and actuarial services to the industry, without which insurance companies could not operate, or indeed could not launch new products.

The Product Life Cycle

The insurance product life cycle is similar, in general, to the product life cycle in manufacturing industries[11]. The length of the cycle depends, however, on the type of risks that the insurance product is supposed to protect against. The type of risk affects both the sales and the shape of the insurance product life curve (figure 8). In particular, the technical and social systems (presented in figure 1 on page 3) affect the insurance product life cycle. Technology does not remove the need for insurance protection, but it can shift the level of sales or reduce its price. For example, if through technology it is possible to reduce the probability of the occurrence of a hazard, then this could dampen the demand for insurance protection or reduce the price at which it is bought. In addition, changes in the social system may bring about the full rejection of certain types of insurance protection. Legislation plays a major role in this respect. Through legislation, the need for workmen compensation insurance protection has become obsolete in many countries. Also, social attitudes can bring the need for an insurance product to an early demise (e.g. the introduction of unemployment benefits, social security benefits and pensions has led to a decline in sales of certain types of insurance products).

In the insurance product life cycle (figure 8) we can identify four major phases: introduction, growth, maturity and decline. The length of each phase (stage) varies according to the type of insurance product, the marketing effort made in relation to that product (i.e. the resources spent on advertising, promotion, distribution/selling and the price policy in operation) and the 'type' of customer (market) at which the insurance product is aimed.

The "introduction" phase in insurance is much shorter than in traditional or ordinary consumer goods. The reason is that insurance products should be introduced and become successful — in terms of units sold — in a relatively short period of time, because the product can be imitated and launched by a competitive insurer. In contrast, the "maturity" phase is longer than with ordinary tangible products.

The analysis of the product life cycle curve in insurance can be carried out by using the Boston Consulting Group approach. This approach is particularly suitable in insurance because most of the insurers offer a mix of insurance programmes, rather than one or two products only. The insurance company has to face the problem of how to allocate resources among the insurance products in its portfolio. The decision is influenced by the rate of growth of the product on one hand and company sales (i.e. the insurer's market share) on the other hand.

Following this approach we can say, therefore, that insurance products which have low growth (i.e. stable sales) and are in mature

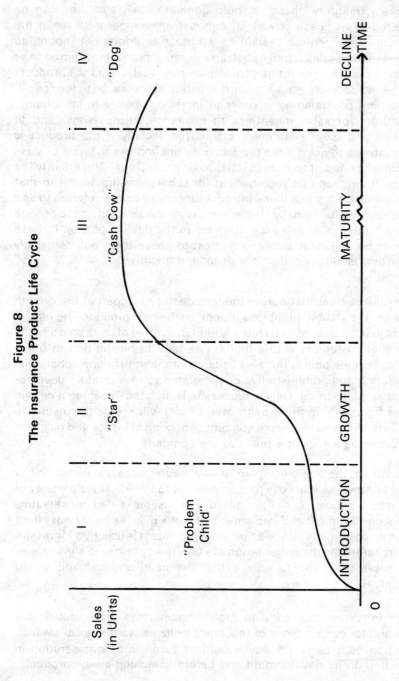

Figure 8
The Insurance Product Life Cycle

Sales
(in Units)

0

INTRODUCTION | GROWTH | MATURITY | DECLINE

TIME

I "Problem Child"

II "Star"

III "Cash Cow"

IV "Dog"

markets (maturity phase), should generate cash and they can be referred to as "cash cows". In contrast, insurance products in the growth stage require marketing efforts (i.e. additional inputs) to increase their sales rapidly; such an insurance product is referred to as "star" because of its future profitability potential. Insurance products in the introductory phase require substantial inputs, both for special marketing programmes in order to increase sales (e.g. advertising, promotion or sales incentives to insurance salespersons) and to sustain and meet customers' claims (particularly if the product is innovatory and risky).If the product does not improve in terms of sales in a short period of time, then it has to be phased out. "Uncertainty" as to its 'future" and its requirement for substantial inputs, mean that the insurance product in the introductory phase can be referred to as a "problem child". Finally, there are insurance products that decline rapidly in terms of sales (i.e. they are in the decline phase). If these cannot be rejuvenated, then it is best to phase them out, as usually their profitability is rather low or indeed negative.

Overall it is clear that during the introductory and part of the growth phases, the insurer might lose money on the new product. The reason is not just because of the relatively limited number of units sold and the fact that customers with a higher risk tend to be the first to buy a particular new policy, but also because of the initial quite substantial marketing and administrative costs related to new product development and launching. Only a successful launch (i.e. reaching a certain sales figure within the growth 'star' phase) will enable the insurer to activate the basic insurance concept of pooling of losses and payment of fortuitous losses at a profit to the company.

To sum up, the insurance plan of one insurer does not usually differ from another, as it is easy for competitors to imitate since patency of assurance policies is not permitted. The insurer is also conservative in his development and implementation of a plan, as he cannot afford to be an opportunist since an insurance contract is usually a long-term affair. Before the implementation of a new policy he has to eliminate all avoidable risks and to ensure that the need and demand would continue.

High inflation, coupled with high interest rates, have shifted the demand for certain types of insurance policies, so the tax allowance position on a certain policy should be taken into consideration in deciding on its development and before launching a new product.

Most of the large insurers produce and offer package policies (i.e. "package deals") at an attractive rate. Lately, the product mix and the business policies of certain insurance companies have been determined by quantitative models aiming to offer in the market place the best mix of product lines, after taking into account both the risks and the rates of return[29].

Another major component of the product element of the marketing mix is the service. Servicing is classified into two types – active and passive. Passive service is what policy holders ask for in the form of *"normal commercial courtesy of prompt and accurate attention to requests for loans, alterations and other enquiries relating to existing business"*[30]. Active service is what policy holders are entitled to expect, but do not always request. The type of service provided by insurers varies widely, but the general criticism is that in pursuing new policy holders, services to existing policy holders are neglected.

One important trend in the development of products to meet customer needs has been the recent growth of the insurance package policy mentioned above which offers within a single contract a diverse range of cover suited to the individual requirements of the customer. A good example of both the marketing research stage and the product development stage of a new insurance package policy can be found in the experience of the Sun Alliance and London Insurance Group[31]. In 1972, Sun Alliance and London had three products on the market: Homeplan, a straightforward buildings and/or contents policy suitable for any segment of the market; Coverplan, a straightforward package policy, providing a package of basic personal insurance covers including contents, all-risks and personal accident, which was intended for the newly-married and the C1 social class markets and the Third Policy, which was intended to cover all those other possessions that the affluent person (the A, B and C1 social classes) has, from gold and diamonds, to pets and golf clubs – he would already have his building and contents insured under Homeplan.

Whereas Coverplan, which was a simple policy for consumers to understand, proved to be very successful, this was not the case for the "up-market" Third Policy. The proposal form for the Third Policy was highly complicated and difficult for consumers to understand. Its obvious failure by 1972 prompted Sun Alliance to reappraise their thinking on how an "up-market" package policy should be developed.

With this in mind, and given that their target market was the upper end of the social scale (A, B, C1's), Sun Alliance embarked on a marketing research programme consisting of a number of surveys to find out what the target market expected from insurance.

In almost every survey carried out, Sun Alliance discovered that one of the insurance problems for respondents in the target market was the complicated nature of both proposal forms and policies. Such complications were the physical difficulty in understanding what the proposal forms and policies were trying to say, the difficulty of establishing whether or not insurance companies were offering the same cover and the complications of establishing where exactly an answer should be written on the proposal form.

From these surveys, Sun Alliance concluded that the basic insurance need of the target market was for simplicity. This meant a straightforward insurance policy, providing the essential covers for a householder's home and personal effects which would be understood by all. In developing such a policy, Sun Alliance decided to offer a policy in six clearly-defined sections, giving the policy holder the choice of which sections he wanted. These were Buildings, Contents, Valuables, Personal Accident, Freezer Contents and Credit Cards. An explanatory booklet to supplement the policy was developed which explained, in terms as plain as was legally possible, each of the six options available in the policy and what was included and excluded in each option. Finally, the proposal form was greatly simplified relative to that of the more traditional package policies such as the Third Policy. One important improvement was that there was now no need to prepare a long tedious list of specified valuables as was the case with previous policies, only those worth over £400 needed to be listed.

Having developed the package policy itself, Sun Alliance turned to the problem of finding a name for it. After conducting a brand name test (i.e. further marketing research) among A, B, C1 potential customers[31] the company finally decided to use the name "Mastercover". Thus, in this way was born a flexible "up-market" package policy geared to satisfying the needs of the A, B, C1 market by providing insurance cover for home and personal effects in a straightforward and uncluttered way.

Product Development Strategies

The insurance product performance depends on four factors[15]: seller concentration, buyer concentration, product differentiation and the conditions of entry.

The number of insurance companies in the U.S.A. is about 2,000, most of them *not* operating on a national basis. In the U.K. there are just under 600 insurance companies, almost every one having one or more subsidiaries. The number of insurance customers is very great. In the U.S.A. over 95% of all families have one or more insurance policies, while in the U.K. about four out of five of all families buy at least one insurance policy – the most popular one being either motor or life insurance.

The insurance product is highly differentiated and a great variety is offered, particularly by the large companies which are very active in *new* product (policy) development. The main reasons for product development cited by insurance companies are:

 i) gaining a competitive advantage;

 ii) stimulating salespersons; and,

 iii) recommendation by an agency department.

The opposition to new product introduction in this industry comes from regulatory legislation (government), consumer attitudes and salespersons' attitudes, but, no doubt, the first of these three obstacles is the most important one. Nevertheless, most of the large U.S. insurance groups develop and launch on average about ten new insurance products yearly. Two principal distinct product development strategies are open to insurance companies:

 i) *The 'Expansion Strategy'.* This consists of the expansion of the services offered within the insurance business, with the aim of increased cross-selling of a wider range of insurance products. This strategy offers an attractive and relatively easy option for most major insurance companies. It would also be expected to bring substantial benefits to the customer by greatly simplifying the task of managing his insurance affairs. A typical insurance customer might at various times in his life need to use a wide range of specialist services in the insurance field.

 The expansion strategy appears to be the main theme of recent product development undertaken by the larger insurance companies which now offer a range of specialist advice on personal business insurance.

 ii) *The 'Differentiation' Strategy.* This involves dividing the core of the insurance product range into packages of services aimed at chosen market segments, with the aim of increasing market share in these segments at the expense of competitors.

In the past many insurance companies have largely pursued a policy of undifferentiated marketing, aiming to appeal to a broad spectrum of customers rather than to particular segments. As a result, the insured sees little difference between the products offered. Attempts to create a degree of product differentiation have been largely unsuccessful, whereas in contrast attempts to increase cross-selling have succeeded.

A move towards differentiated marketing requires the development of distinct products aimed at chosen market segments. For promotional purposes the core of such a product would consist of a group of services selected as being of particular relevance to the segment. One might, for example, envisage insurance packages aimed specifically at the affluent, the student, the young married couple, the retired, the shopkeeper, the farmer, the small businessman, the international traveller and so on.

A strategy of product differentiation might be accompanied by a contraction of the service range, if efforts are to be concentrated on only a few market segments. Abandoning irrelevant services would help to control costs, allowing a service which has been stripped of irrelevances to be offered at a highly competitive price.

To sum up, in planning services/product strategies there are four alternatives open to the insurance company, as indicated in Table 6:

1. Offering more of *existing services to existing customers* – i.e. market penetration (e.g. increasing the amount of life or medical insurance, per customer).

2. Offering more of *existing services to new customers* – i.e. market development (e.g. selling existing insurance policies, say motor insurance, to new drivers/car owners).

3. Developing *new services/products to existing customers* – i.e. service/product development (e.g. identifying a certain insurance need, say, dental insurance and offering it to existing customers).

4. Developing *new services for new customers* – i.e. diversification (e.g. going into new, more risky, ventures, say, offering insurance policies to hang gliding customers).

Table 6
Planning Insurance Product Strategies

Customers / Products	Existing	New
Existing	(1) MARKET PENETRATION (e.g. increasing the amount of medical or life insurance)	(2) MARKET DEVELOPMENT (e.g. selling additional insurance products, say life assurances, to newly-weds)
New	(3) PRODUCT/SERVICES DEVELOPMENT (e.g. offering a new product, say dental insurance to existent customers)	(4) DIVERSIFICATION (i.e. developing new insurance products for new customers, e.g. accident insurance for hang gliding customers)

The development of new insurance products should be based on a thorough analysis of the market. There are four ways of developing insurance products. Firstly, the insurer can follow a policy of market extension (or development) through the development of new policies and programmes designed to meet more precisely the needs of various customer segments. Secondly, the insurer can recognise that its facilities can offer opportunities for implementing a strategy of product extension (e.g. provide special insurance schemes). Thirdly, the insurer can pursue product extension policies, implemented through the development of new insurance products. Fourthly, the insurer may follow a policy of conglomerate growth (or diversification) by establishing insurance services (where regulations permit) which are complementary to existing operations and are likely to further the use of other insurance services.

CHAPTER SEVEN

PRICING

The price of an insurance policy is a prime consideration for most customers, except professional insurance buyers and financial institutions. Indeed in the U.S.A. about 45% of all insurance customers ask about price at two or more insurance companies before making a decision on car insurance, while 35% change agents for a 10% change in price and 50% of the customers change agents for an 18% change in price.[32].

Broadly speaking, the prices of insurance policies are calculated by taking into account several major factors: the probability of claims (risk assessment), operating costs, the expected rate of inflation and its bearing on costs and finally the level of competition in prices. In addition to setting the premiums, pricing also concerns itself with the manner in which these premiums are paid. Premium payments can either be a lump sum, annual, bi-annual, quarterly, monthly or weekly, depending, of course, on the nature and duration of the policy and on the financial circumstances of the policy holder.

The Objectives of Pricing in Insurance

The supplier of insurance should have two main marketing objectives as far as the price setting is concerned:

i) to attract as many customers as possible from the selected segments; and,

ii) to do this under the most profitable conditions.

This does not necessarily mean that he should price according to the cost of servicing the customer. In the life assurance industry, an important distinction should be made between "profit" and "surplus". Surplus is important as it serves as a reserve (or stock) for losses in following years.

One should remember that the objective of pricing is *not* to make the same absolute or percentage profit on each policy sold, *but rather to make as much profit as possible, within the constraints of continuing activity in the long run.* This cannot be done unless an insurance company has reliable information on three factors:

i) the nature of demand facing the insurance company in each segment for each type of product and the price which the potential customers are "willing to pay";

ii) the price levels charged by rival or competing insurance companies; and,

iii) knowledge of the full cost of supplying the full insurance cover, as in the *long run*, an insurance company will not be able to survive if the price is lower than its full costs.

Price tactics in insurance should be used to exploit different price sensitivities. For example, compare the insurance premiums which can be obtained by a company like Ford for a life insurance policy for its employees, with the price (premiums) at which the very same policy will be offered to an individual Ford employee by an ordinary insurance company. However, to charge discriminatory prices in this way successfully, there must be no inter-segment leakage. Insurance product differences also permit the charging of different prices which are not proportional to the "production" costs of such differentiation. Insurance product development might enable the use of price as a flexible, useful tool in increasing a company's profitability. However, promotion, advertising and distribution are also important tools which can effectively assist in increasing the profitability, since promotion and advertising can appeal to preferences in such a way that discriminatory pricing becomes possible. Commercial Union, for example, can perhaps charge a higher premium for the 'same' insurance cover, due to the certain 'image' which this insurance company has created around its special insurance services.

Pricing policies in insurance, based on marketing research and actuarial findings, have led to the development of several different pricing approaches such as credit life insurance, quantity discounts, lower rates for women, lower individual rates in group insurances, ease of payment programmes (including automatic salary deduction of premiums) or special rate discounts (where actuarial data provides a sound base for such a price strategy) to non-drinkers (for car and life insurance), safe drivers (for those taking advanced driving training) or non-smokers, etc. In order to facilitate a better service, the process of dealing with claims has been speeded up and certain insurance companies in the U.S.A. offer drive-in claim facilities, where advance payments are made on the spot.

Price differentials in the insurance market are quite noticeable and warrant some mention. The insurance market when defined in an economic sense is, or should be, a perfect market; a market with a large number of companies in the industry, all offering a "homogeneous" product. Entry is relatively free and easy and consumers have perfect knowledge of the market so that it should be quite difficult for any company in the industry to charge prices drastically different from the rest without either making a loss or pricing itself out of the market. Until fairly recently, the last qualification (perfect knowledge) did not really apply to the insurance market. This "uninformed market" characteristic coupled with the fact that insurance is sold not bought, accounts for any existing price differentials[33]. In this market, the buyer does not approach a perfect market and offer his custom to a particular company for a product obtainable at a similar price from any other company within the industry. In place of such action, the buyer is approached by the seller who tries to sell the product. It is not very often that the buyer is approached by various sellers, thus being given the chance to compare prices, but this is gradually changing for the better with the advance in technology, thus making it possible to obtain such information in comfort (e.g. on a television screen).

Insurance buying is becoming more and more price dependent. The trend is towards competitive pricing, but even then a number of other factors have to be considered. Inflation is one of those factors and presents a few problems. The insured no doubt would very much like the amount contracted now to be of some real value at the time it matures, but in view of ever-rising inflation this is hardly likely to be the case. The way to get round the problem would be a continuous adjustment of the premiums to keep up with inflation. However, customers might simply avoid the inflation problem by not entering into *any* insurance contracts, where the purchasing power of money is expected to go down[34].

Attitude questionnaires, whereby the seller attempts to assess the prospect's attitude towards pricing insurance policy values and related topics, have recently been undertaken. Results from the few companies that have tried attitude questionnaires as a means towards more accurate pricing have proved the procedure useful[32] and adoption of these by more insurance sectors should be very beneficial.

Ratemaking

There are four major elements in any pricing policy decision in insurance:

i) *Costs.* Insurers use two instruments through which they try to approximate their costs based on the historical experience of a

control group to that of a present consumer segment for which an insurance price/cost prediction is being made. These two instruments are:
a) rating; and,
b) underwriting.

Through rating, insurers try to predict the expected losses of a market segment from the historical loss experience of a group with similar characteristics.

ii) *The price that the customers are "willing" to pay.* This depends on their income, socio-economic class, background, tastes and preferences. The price that a customer might be willing to pay for a certain insurance product can be found by a market survey or a market study.

iii) *Government legislation and taxation policy.* This factor might also affect both costs and the price that an insurance customer will be willing to pay in order to avoid confrontation with the law (e.g. motor insurance).

iv) *Competitors' prices.* In formulating pricing policies for existent insurance products, companies tend to take into consideration the prices of existent products offered by competing companies.

Insurance pricing is also called *ratemaking* and has several objectives:

i) Rates should be adequate (i.e. high enough to "cover" all expenses, meet all claims and leave a fair profit to the insurer).

ii) Rates must be competitive, simple to understand and stable. This is one of the reasons why insurers have difficulties in raising premiums in inflationary periods, despite rises in costs.

iii) In addition to operational costs (e.g. administrative expenses and commissions), insurance companies must take into consideration other costs such as fraudulent and/or inflated claims.

Basically, there are 3 types of insurance pricing (or ratemaking) methods as presented in figure 9.

1) *Class Rating*

This is pricing based on the average loss in the same class. The assumption here is that future average losses will be influenced by a similar set of variables for the same type of insured (e.g. in life

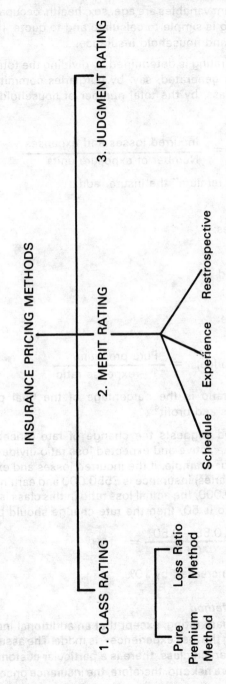

Figure 9
The Major Methods of Insurance Pricing (Ratemaking)

INSURANCE PRICING METHODS

1. CLASS RATING

Pure Premium Method

Loss Ratio Method

2. MERIT RATING

Schedule

Experience

Restrospective

3. JUDGMENT RATING

insurance the important variables are age, sex, health, occupation and life style). Class rating is simple to calculate and to quote. It is used particularly in motor and household insurance.

The premium in class rating is determined by dividing the total losses and costs per annum generated, say, by burglaries committed in a given underwriting class, by the total number of households in the same class, i.e.:

$$\text{Pure Premium} \quad = \quad \frac{\text{Incurred losses and expenses}}{\text{Number of exposure units}}$$

On top of the "pure premium" the insurer adds:

  i) commissions;

 ii) overhead expenses;

iii) company taxes;

iv) contingencies; and,

 v) profits,

to determine the price:

$$\text{Final Premium (price)} \quad = \quad \frac{\text{Pure premium}}{1 - \text{expense ratio}}$$

where the expense ratio is the percentage of the final premium available for expenses and profit[9].

The loss ratio method suggests the change of rate (price) by the difference between the active and expected loss ratio divided by the expected loss ratio. For example, if the incurred losses and expenses from household (burglaries) insurance is £550,000 and earnings (past premiums) are £1,000,000, the actual loss ratio in this class is 0.55. If the expected loss ratio is 50, then the rate change should be

$$\frac{0.55 - 0.50}{0.50} = 10\%$$

i.e. the rate must be increased by 10%.

2) The Merit Rating Method

This is similar to the class rating, except that an additional individual adjustment – recording the loss experience – is made. The assumption here is that, within a certain class, there is a particular customer who carries significantly more risk and, therefore, the insurance price for him should be adjusted accordingly. As indicated in figure 9, there are three methods of insurance pricing under this category: schedule, experience and retrospective rating.

Schedule rating is used mainly in commercial building insurance and is based on an individual analysis of the characteristics of the various objects to be insured (e.g. use, occupancy, maintenance and other similar aspects related to the future protection of individual buildings). Schedule rating encourages expenditure on self-protective devices by the customer.

Experience rating is based on previous loss experience with a particular customer. However, it is used only with large customers, where the insurer would like to offer a "fair" and competitive rate in order not to lose a major account (e.g. in commercial motor insurance).

The retrospective rating method attempts to reflect the insured loss experience during the *current* period. This approach suggests a maximum and minimum premium, depending on the *actual* losses during the current insurance period. Retrospective insurance pricing is used in fixing prices for burglary and general liability insurance.

3) *Judgment Rating*
This is a method of pricing used when a class (i.e. a standard or type) rate cannot be calculated because the risk is relatively diverse (e.g. in marine or airline insurance). In those circumstances, the premiums are a result of expert judgment.

Carter[16] suggests that a full cost pricing is the method that generally prevails in pricing the insurance product on both sides of the Atlantic. Insurers fix the premiums rates in relation to:

a) costs (i.e. claims plus commissions plus expenses); and,

b) profits.

There are, however, difficulties in correctly forecasting the expected costs (particularly claims) on the one hand and future earnings from premiums (sales) investment, on the other hand. This uncertainty affects the overall profitability of many insurers and represents the major reason for many bankruptcies in this industry.

Pricing of Life Assurances
According to Brennan[35], the determination of life insurance policy premiums involves three basic elements: mortality, interest and expenses. However, mortality, or the expected life of the policy-holder, is the major factor to consider when pricing life insurance.

The first step in evaluating a proposal for life insurance from a respondent is for the company to estimate how long that respondent will live. This prediction is made by taking two factors into account. Firstly, the relevant personal information supplied on the proposal form and, secondly, the latest empirical studies on mortality within the sector of the population to which the respondent belongs. A prediction of how long the intended policy holder is expected to live enables the insurance company to forecast the eventual claim against that policy, although the forecasting of such a claim involves taking into account a further element — the rate of interest.

Let us assume that the claim is a fixed sum in money terms, as is the case in many life insurance policies. By estimating the number of years the respondent is expected to live and by predicting what the rate of interest will be over those years (i.e. economic forecasting), the insurance company will be able to discount the money value of the claim over the estimated period of life expectancy by the predicted rates of interest, to arrive at the present value of the claim. Naturally, the longer the period of life expectancy of the respondent, the lower will be the present value of the claim.

The present value of the claim represents the present value of what the company will eventually pay out against the policy. It, therefore, represents the present cost to the company of issuing that policy. Once calculated, the present cost of the policy is the basis from which the premium or price of the policy is determined. If the present cost of the policy is high (i.e. if the life expectancy of the respondent is low), then the premium will be very high. Inversely, if the present cost is low (i.e. if life expectancy is high), then the premium will be relatively low. Of course, if the present cost of the policy is too high (i.e. if the life expectancy of the respondent is very low — if he, for instance, is a lion-tamer, or is simply very old), then the company may refuse insurance outright.

So far then, we have said that the twin factors of mortality and interest determine the present value of the claim against a life insurance policy, that the present value of the claim represents the present cost of issuing that policy and that the present cost of the policy is the basis from which the premium rate for the policy is determined.

However, the premium rate is not only a function of the present cost of the policy. In other words, it does not depend purely on mortality and interest. It is also necessary to include in the premium a loading factor for the administrative and maintenance expenses incurred by the company in preparing and distributing the policy and the general running of their business. Operating expenses, therefore, constitute a further element, in addition to risk and interest, in determining the premium for life assurance.

Of the three basic elements in pricing life insurance mortality, interest and expenses — the only one which is under the control of insurance management is expenses. The other two — mortality and interest — are, of course, respectively demographic and economic factors outside management influence. Thus, by strictly controlling the operating expenses of the company through increased administrative efficiency, insurance management will be in a position to bring about a marginal reduction in premium rates, thus making their policies more attractive in the intensely competitive life insurance market. Other means of making policies competitive include the structuring of premium payments in a fashion which is convenient to the policy holder. For instance, a company may allow wage-earning policy holders to pay weekly, even though this may entail extra administrative effort.

The competitive nature of the life assurance industry and the fluctuating rate of inflation tend to affect the premiums of insurance policies. Most companies try as much as possible to keep their premiums as low as possible. In life assurance, rates charged are based on mortality tables selected from the best available actuarial studies. Usually, the life assurance companies try to set their premiums at a sufficiently competitive level, so that other companies cannot offer the same benefits at a significantly lower premium. Even if there were not competition, good business sense suggests that a company would not sell very much insurance if its premiums were unreasonably high.

Besides being reasonable, the premiums for life assurance must also be adequate in the sense that they must be sufficient, with investments, to pay the benefits promised, as well as cover the expenses of operating the plan. In addition, the premiums must be equitable and fair. Thus, consideration must be given to such factors as the sex, age, health and occupation of the persons whose lives are to be insured. The same or very similar benefits cannot ethically be offered to one policy holder at one premium rate and to another at a different rate, unless there are variations in risk or expenses to justify the difference. Most life companies would follow this principle as a matter of good business practice alone, but discrimination among the insured of the same demographic and risk class is prohibited by law.

The market is also price conscious and many publications are now available which compare the past performance of given policies amongst life assurance companies, to give the potential customer a greater opportunity to find a policy with the best projected value for the premium paid.

There are many different types of premium systems. The most common is the level premium system mentioned above, whereby the premium remains constant for as long as it is payable. This is a technique adopted by the insurance industry in an attempt to minimise adverse selection and at the same time make it financially feasible for policy holders to continue their protection even to advanced ages[36]. Under this system, the policy holder has to pay a higher premium (relative to mortality costs, expenses and profits) in the early years, to offset the inadequacy of premiums in the later policy years.

Another type of premium is the net single premium, whereby the premium is payable in a single sum at the time the policy is issued. However, under this scheme, the amount of life assurance purchased would be seriously limited. Besides, most people cannot afford to pay a very large single premium for a life assurance policy. Therefore, allowances have been made for the payment to be made in smaller quarterly, monthly or annual premiums. This scheme is known as the net level annual premium. This type of premium is computed to produce, for example, sufficient amounts to pay all the death claims as they are represented, if death occurs in accordance with the mortality table used and if interest is earned at the rate assumed. However, this type of premium does not make any allowance for such factors as the expenses of running the company, the possibility that there would be more deaths in some years than those shown by the table or that a lower rate of interest might actually be earned. To provide for these as well as other factors, an addition known as "the loading" is made to the net premium. The result is the gross annual premium which is the amount the policy holder actually pays.

To sum up, pricing in insurance is very much affected by risk probability, operating costs, level of competition and the rate of inflation. Overall, there is a tendency towards more accurate pricing. This is the net result of a growing sophistication in forecasting of claims. In addition, the incidence of larger companies, usually through mergers, may — in the long run — lead to a decrease in competition, lower costs and therefore lower prices. However, in the short run, the recent higher inflationary pressures tend to lead to higher costs and, therefore, higher prices.

Presently, the methods of payment of premiums by policy holders are on an annual, half yearly, monthly and weekly basis. In view of the rising costs of administration, it has been suggested that the weekly and monthly basis of payment should be discouraged by fixing a progressive rate of premium for such payments.

During the last few years there has been an increasing realisation of the inter-relationships amongst pricing, distribution, advertising, promotion and insurance product development policies. For this reason, it might well be a very damaging mistake to employ the price tool on its own. In order to overcome this difficulty, several very large companies have recently considered employing multivariate methods such as the N.M.S. (Nonmetric Multidimensional Scaling) to assess the importance and relative effectiveness of the various alternative marketing tools (e.g. straight discounts, credit, price reduction campaigns, "better services", more promotion, more advertising, larger margins to distributors/agents or longer lines — i.e. a greater variety of insurance products/services offered) which the company should employ in order to find out the right and most optimal combination (or mix) of these marketing tools. One should emphasise that each of the above tools have a *cost* that must ultimately be reflected in the insurance product's price and lead — eventually — to a certain result in terms of demand and profitability which must be justified. While most of these N.M.S. studies have been carried out in industrial and consumer goods markets, they can potentially be applied in the insurance industry as well[20].

CHAPTER EIGHT

ADVERTISING AND PROMOTION

After the needs of the insurance market have been identified through market research and policies to meet these needs have been developed, then the price or premium for these policies must be determined, as shown in the previous chapter. The next stage in the insurance marketing programme is to advertise and promote these policies to potential customers.

General Functions of Advertising in the Insurance Industry

Advertising in the insurance business can be said to work in two principal ways. Firstly, it contributes towards market expansion by bringing to the attention of the public some insurance products which could be very beneficial to customers. The second function of advertising stems from its ability to persuade the public that one company's products are better than the products of other companies and, therefore, that they should be purchased in preference, thus expanding that particular company's business as opposed to that of its competitors. Insurance companies could also employ advertising to educate the public about the significance of insurance packages and products in general.

Before advertising, however, the company has to establish consumer requirements, usage, behaviour, attitudes and decisions about insurance products. Consumer needs are then determined and ways are devised to make the consumer aware of a particular product and its benefits.

Advertising could be undertaken through various channels (e.g. television, newspapers and professional journals). Each of these has certain advantages and disadvantages (Table 7). Television is advantageous in that it is both audio and visual and, therefore, presents its message actively. The message is put across through pictures and supportive speech, so certain desirable points are easily emphasised and, hopefully, make some lasting impact on the consumer — long enough for him to make an enquiry. The disadvantage is that the message can only last for a few seconds and can be very costly. Newspaper and journal advertising can only be directed at certain segments of the community — those people expected to read those particular papers and journals. Advertisement posters can also be placed on buses and trains and in public places like airport terminals, train stations or cinemas, but inevitably these can only be general in nature.

Table 7

Characteristics of the Various Promotional Channels in Insurance

Characteristics \ Channels	Television	Newspaper	Magazine	Cinema	Posters	Direct Mail
Coverage	Wide	Very wide, however rather specialised	Smaller and to specific market segment(s)	Wide – but mostly for the younger generation	Very wide	Limited
Transmission	Active	Passive	Passive	Active	Passive	Active
Impact	Colour, sound and movement make impact strong	Not very impressive; quite dull without colour	Sometimes colour given to impress target market	As with TV	Strong	Quite strong
Amount of information	Very little information given to prospects	Considerable information carried in daily newspapers	As with newspapers	Little information	Usually little unexplained message	Full information provided
Flexibility of insertions and cancellations	Flexible	Quite flexible but may need time for notice	As with newspapers	Booking in advance	Book suitable space	Very flexible
Repetition required	Regular	Very frequent in local newspapers	Depends on the frequency of the magazine	Infrequent	Constant repetition	Infrequent
Retention	Very short	Lasts long	Lasts long	Short	Short	Lasts long
Costs	Very costly	Less costly than TV	Less costly than TV	High	Cheap	Expensive (but efficient)

Insurance companies try to enhance their image also through promotional techniques like sponsoring sports, assisting charity organisations and the like. In addition, they give small gifts to policy holders through the agents, aimed at creating a favourable image in the minds of the customers contacted.

Changes in life style have had some considerable effect on insurance marketing. Improved communication systems have made immobility a thing of the past. People move because of family contacts, better job prospects or current job commitments. This has made it necessary for insurance companies to try and retain the custom of their clients when they move to a different location. To do this, they utilise the services of direct marketing; they use direct mail to maintain contact with policy holders and their agents find this method useful in developing enquiries, qualifying prospects and following up on established clients. Companies also use this method to maintain their image in the minds of their customers. In short, direct mail, coupled with personal contact, can be very effective, both as a means of promotion and distribution.

Insurance advertising is normally conducted through the mass media such as television, newspapers, popular magazines, street posters and commercial radio and is backed up by promotional activity mainly conducted through insurance sales representatives who seek out clients and offer advice and assistance to help them choose the policies best suited to their needs. Let us examine this process in more detail, referring firstly to advertising and secondly to promotion, bearing in mind that, in practice, both functions are highly interrelated.

For a company wishing to advertise consumer insurance on a national scale, the two major media are the press and television. Press advertising is conducted through national daily and Sunday newspapers, popular weekly magazines and specialist magazines such as *Autocar* for car insurance, for example.

Television is an immensely powerful advertising medium and is becoming increasingly preferred by insurance companies as a means of putting across to the public a direct and vivid message of the benefits of insurance. However, according to Winterbottom[37], television as an insurance advertising medium suffers from three distinct disadvantages:

i) Its cost is very high which means that an effective campaign, with any frequency, calls for a bigger advertising budget than most advertisers in the insurance market are often prepared to support.

In fact, according to O'Reilly[38], the advertising budgets of insurance companies are very small in relation to the size of their assets.

ii) It can provide only a very short message. A 30 second commercial is a very brief length of time to deal with a subject as complicated as insurance.

iii) The third and probably the greatest disadvantage is that television is a difficult medium from which to get a direct response. If an insurance company is spending money to persuade T.V. viewers to buy its product, it wants to be sure that it is its own brand, and not that of competitors, which gets the benefit. This problem is partly overcome in press advertising, because normally a coupon is included in the advertisement, which enables an interested reader to contact the insurance company direct for further information and assistance.

A comparison of some major insurance advertising media is presented on table 7.

In order to ensure that television, and similar forms of "no-response" advertising such as street posters, actually result in sales of the advertiser's own brand, it is necessary that such advertising is backed up by promotional activity on the part of the company's sales representatives. This promotional activity, as performed by sales-persons, takes the form of searching out potential clients, mainly through personal contact, and is at its most effective immediately after a national T.V. advertising campaign when the company's name is still fresh in people's minds. Promotional goals might be very diverse and include not just advertising, but also building or maintaining image as presented in figure 10.

Prospecting: How to Obtain Customers

The method by which an insurance salesperson can seek out potential customers is known in the insurance trade as *prospecting*. The *Insurance Mail*[33] defines prospecting as *"a planned searching process"*. The object of this search is, of course, a potential client or, in other words, a "prospect". There are various prospecting methods through which, for example, the life insurance salesperson can seek out potential clients, but perhaps the most rewarding, if carried out successfully, is the method known as *Situation Prospecting*.

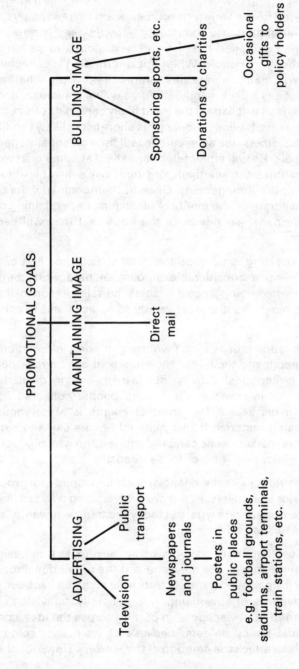

Figure 10
Some Major Promotional Goals in Insurance

Situation prospecting is where the salesperson compiles a long list of people, gathered from a variety of sources, such as newspapers, trade journals, social gatherings, community activities and business promotions. Having compiled this list, the next step is to gather some information about the people. When this information is collected, the salesperson will then evaluate this information, to see whether any particular person is a likely candidate for, say, life insurance. In doing so, the salesperson will extract the most likely candidates from the list and discard the rest. Having produced his short-list of likely candidates or potential customers, the salesperson will then personally approach these individuals. He will either telephone them at home or at work to make an appointment to see them, or simply pay a direct visit to their home without prior arrangement. Once in their company, the salesperson can elaborate on the merits of life insurance, explaining how it will meet their particular needs, in the hope that they will become policy holders.

Situation prospecting is perhaps the most difficult method of prospecting, involving a considerable amount of hard work, but it is certainly highly-rewarding since it enables the salesperson to uncover life insurance needs from a great variety of sources and to act upon these needs.

In so far as situation prospecting involves gathering information on a long list of people and their insurance needs, it can be regarded not merely as a promotional activity, but also as a form of marketing research. All the information on various people collected by the salesperson in his search for potential clients is a storehouse of valuable research material. If this material is carefully and expertly analysed, future market needs can be identified and new products can be developed in anticipation of these needs.

Among the institutions in the financial sector, insurers as a group are one of the major advertisers. In the past, advertising was passive and of the prestige or corporate type, but today the trend is towards "sales-orientated" insurance advertising.

The three most important aspects of an advertising campaign in insurance are: the media, the message and the promotional tools, as shown earlier in figure 4 on page 20. Very little research has been done on the effectiveness of advertising, but, generally, television advertising is preferred to newspapers, in putting across the idea/concept to the potential policy holders, because of its music, colour and movement which attack the emotion of the viewers. However, the fact is that apart from life assurance, insurance products are very seldom sold by advertising alone, probably because they are intangible plus the fact that in the case of general insurance, the reader who might be attracted by, say, a newspaper advertisement will have forgotten all about it by the time his existing policy is due for renewal (although this might not be the case for the first-time buyer). The failures on the part of advertisement campaigns have also further emphasised this point.

The media used widely by insurance companies include newspaper advertising, window display, poster display on billboards, buses, trains and underground stations. All these are relatively cheaper than television and are designed to keep a company's name before the public. Drop leaflets are also inserted into magazines and are used to obtain sales from a selected area, while direct mail is used primarily by insurance companies to keep their agents posted on the latest plans, because advertising in itself is ineffective unless it is followed up by advice, explanation and action from the sales representatives.

On the promotional side, small gift items like calendars, diaries, blotters and memo pads are provided by the insurers to the agents for distribution to potential policy holders. In addition, attractive standardised prospectuses which contain the main policy conditions and premium rates are given to agents to aid them in their sales.

Most of the insurance agents spend their time between travelling, persuading clients and desk work in their offices. Because travelling, prospecting and obtaining new clients is crucial, it is very important to give the right amount of attention to planning. In order to facilitate a systematic approach to prospecting and still to be able to keep in touch with existing customers without long intervals of time elapsing between calls, a system called the "salesperson wheel" can be put into operation.

The approach consists of dividing the salesperson's area of operation (territory) into four parts which, while being similar in size, are geographically different. This facilitates time economies and reduces travelling costs. Each day the salesperson will visit a different area (e.g. area 1 on Monday, area 2 on Tuesday and so on, being back to area 1 on Friday, area 2 on the following Monday, etc.). The advantages of this approach are:

i) concentration of activity in one territory, saving travelling time and 'enforcing' some planning of the sale method(s) to be employed, itinerary, etc.; and,

ii) the salesperson will operate in *two* different territories (areas) every week — thus enabling him/her to keep in touch with prospects that might not be available for contact on a certain day of the week.

This approach is particularly efficient in selling life assurance policies, although it may of course have practical use in the cross-selling of other insurance policies as well.

Advertising Life Assurance Policies

In order to encourage the public to buy life assurance, persuasion has to be used. The most obvious and effective way would be to employ salesmen to knock on the door of every household. However, this method is impractical and costly. So, the best method to reach the public is through advertisements.

Ten years ago the only form of advertising used by the life insurance companies was designed to establish their image, particularly through the insurance press. This has now changed. Advertising has become a major method of marketing used to expand the market by obtaining a direct response from the public. Furthermore, it helps to generate business for a company and aids in its expansion by persuading the public to buy its products in preference to its competitors'.

Most life assurance companies advertise through the press — mainly daily and Sunday newspapers and magazines of general interest, like *Newsweek*. Advertisements which appear in the press take many forms and include advertisements incorporating a proposal form, as well as display advertising simply designed to keep the name of a particular life assurance company in the public's mind. In addition, some advertisements relate to a particular type of life assurance or alternatively are directed at a particular group of consumers. Occasionally, rather than having the advertisements printed on the pages of magazines, pamphlets are inserted into magazines. This is a cheaper form of advertisement and enables a wider distribution of pamphlets

The television is an immensely powerful medium for advertising, but as far as the advertising of life assurance is concerned, it has certain disadvantages as noted earlier in this chapter. Furthermore, an advertiser will have no indication as to whether the advertisements benefited him or his competitors. For although an advertisement on the television might spark off a viewer's interest in acquiring a life assurance policy, it does not guarantee that the interested viewer will approach the company that placed the advertisement. Instead, he might approach another company.

Due to the unsuitability of using television advertisements, some television contractors are working hard to come up with schemes to provide facilities such as instant telephone contact through which the interested viewer can respond. At present, however, this problem has not been solved satisfactorily and is not likely to be so for some time.

Presently, banks and credit card companies also play a role in advertising life assurance policies. For example, the National Westminster Bank sends out application forms for purchasing life assurance policies to clients together with the invoices for Access.

Sometimes, satisfied clients also play a role in advertising for a particular company by making the company known to friends and relatives.

Life assurance products, however, are not promoted solely by press, television and other forms of advertisements. Rather, life offices also print and publish promotional material designed intentionally for use by potential customers.

Apart from the consumer advertising mentioned above, there is also the area of specialist or trade advertising, whereby the sales representatives are kept up to date with new products by the provision of new promotional material. In addition, brokers are also given literature designed to inform and persuade them to promote a particular company's policies. Further promotional material for brokers and agents includes calendars, diaries and stationery.

CHAPTER NINE

CHANNELS OF DISTRIBUTION

Distribution refers mainly to the type of channel employed, its uses and advantages and disadvantages to the marketing of insurance services. It plays an important role in the marketing of insurance since the industry very much depends on intermediaries to sell a significant proportion of its products. Distribution channels are among the most critical decisions in insurance marketing management, because they affect almost every other marketing decision (e.g. pricing and advertising), so they exercise a powerful influence on the rest of the marketing mix. Similarly, decisions on distribution channels quite often involve the insurance company in long-term commitments to other companies (i.e. reinsurers) or customers.

Insurance distribution channels are of two main types – *direct* marketing channels, whereby intermediaries employed by the insurer solicit the insurer's products and *indirect* marketing channels, whereby intermediaries not employed by the insurer offer supposedly impartial advice and recommendations to the public.

Direct Marketing Channels

Direct marketing channels are distribution systems within which the insurance company deals directly with the insured through its own employees by the following methods (figure 11):

1) *Direct Mail*
This method is used to solicit sales from special markets such as, for example, term life assurance contracts from university students. It reduces operational costs and is ideal for simple contracts which require very little or no underwriting as the applicant can complete the proposal form which is included in the catalogue/mail.

Direct mail as a channel of distribution has become quite useful in insurance, especially in the recent past. It is not only a means through which the company maintains contact with policy holders, but also for selling group and association plans and other individual businesses to new customers. Changes in life style have affected the insurance market just as they have in many other markets. For instance, better communications have eased mobility which quite often means breaking ties with a local agent. Mailing then comes to the fore in an attempt to maintain contact between the company and client.

Direct mailing also makes it possible to segment the huge total insurance market into smaller and more uniform groups of consumers.

This obviously contributes to efficiency. Until recently, market segmentation in the insurance industry tended to be based mostly on geographic and demographic factors. Now segmentation, besides the two bases just mentioned, is becoming more psychographic as well[27] (e.g. segmentation by habits, attitudes, life styles or professions).

Mailing as a means of distribution is gaining ground because of its relative ease of getting into contact with those customers who would otherwise be left out. However, in order to ensure that the method is really effective, it has to have some personal contact as a back-up.

2) *Prospecting*

As mentioned in the previous chapter, this is a major source of sales, although often the public approaches the insuring company direct for their needs. Some companies are gradually encouraging this means of selling insurance contracts as it involves no intermediaries, so no commission payouts and the client definitely receives different treatment (e.g. some concessions might be made on the rates of the premiums).

3) *Full Time Company Sales Staff*

These are highly-trained professional sales representatives, employed by the large majority of insurance companies all over the world. Their primary concern is with selling their employer's whole range of policies, either through brokers and other intermediaries, or directly to the public. In their direct dealings with clients, insurance salespersons will offer advice and assistance to help them choose the policies best suited to their requirements. Through this personal contact with customers, the salespersons, by asking questions, will pick up a great deal of information concerning the needs and preferences of customers which will then be fed back to the insurance company and used as market intelligence.

The customer may be in a slightly safer situation dealing with the company's salaried employee than with an independent agent or a broker who, because of the commission element, may actually be more interested in another 'sale' rather than in giving proper advice and help. The latter may even coerce the not-so-well-informed client into some contract which may not really serve his needs. (On the other hand, the broker's duty is to advise his clients about the range of products on the market, whilst the salaried official will only mention the products.)

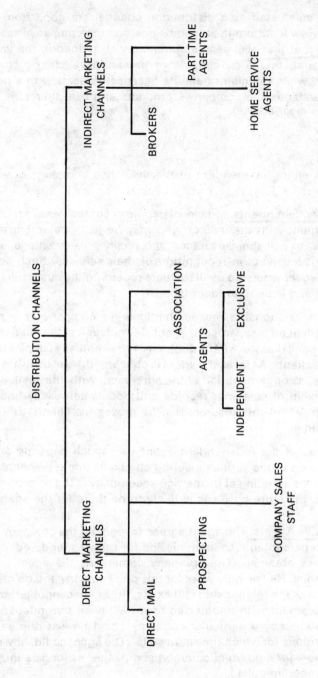

Figure 11

Direct vs Indirect Distribution Channels in Insurance

Company sales staff as a distribution channel are good from both points of view (i.e. from the insurer's position the company is at least confident that they will secure someone well trained in the various products and, therefore, capable of presenting a clear picture to prospects, while the client benefits because he deals with a person who understands the company's products and can, therefore, offer sound and clear advice).

4) *Agents*

These are either independent of the insurance company, or wholly owned by it.

i) Independent Agents. Individual people or companies enter into an agreement with the insurer who may be just one among many others to sell their insurance and receive a percentage of the amount involved, in recognition of their services. Such agents have legal ownership of all the data regarding the customers (e.g. policy and expiration records).

Such a relationship makes the insuring company very much dependent on that particular agent. Termination of the relationship could spell disaster for the company and eventually culminate in a loss of clients. As far as the agent is concerned, he usually has little to lose, as on termination of the agreement with the insurer, his ownership of customer records and details can easily find him custom with other insurers (i.e. he moves his clients to a new company).

Success of the independent agent very much depends on the reputation of the various insuring companies he represents. The higher the standing of the particular company in the opinion of the public, the more business is likely to be there for the agent.

ii) Exclusive Agents. The agent agrees to work for the company for a certain percentage (i.e. commission for services rendered) of the business obtained. The company commands the agent's total allegiance. He can only work for this one company and no others. As long as the relationship still exists, the agent cannot enter into an agreement with another company — unlike the independent agent whereby a particular company could be just one among many others for which the agent sells. (The agent could, however, also work for a group of common companies, as long as they are under one umbrella.)

Policy records and expiration information is legally owned by the insuring company. In this kind of relationship, it is the agent who stands in a precarious position. Termination of the relationship very often means a total loss of business for the agent, but it is very easy for the company to go out and look for another agent to carry on the service.

There should be an optimal number of agents chosen by a company to work for it and a non-exclusive agent should also have an optimal number of companies which he represents. The policy of "the more the agents/companies – the more business", may not work due to complexities of large numbers. Lack of confidence from both sides could result due to poor communications between the agent and company due to size. This lack of communication could easily result in conflicting actions which could be disastrous to a company's marketing strategy.

Agents are the means through which the marketing strategy of an insurance company is effected, so liaison with the agents in developing strategy and products by the insurer is an important factor that should not be overlooked. Agents play an important part also in influencing new product developments. In their capacity as go-betweens, agents can greatly contribute towards marketing strategy development through the following activities:

a) Identifying target markets and making recommendations on the type of products and services to satisfy the needs of that particular market segment.

b) Supplying ideas on product innovations obtained through contact with clients.

c) Expressing opinions (again gathered through contact with clients) about the likely effect of any price changes.

d) Pointing out shortcomings in customer service – made aware to him, of course, through his direct contact.

Given the necessary help and support from the insurers, agents can contribute much to the company's marketing programme. Assistance to the agents from the company can be given by:

a) Providing information obtained through research on existing clients and potential customers.

b) Taking part in the selection and training of agency employees – although this may be more applicable to exclusive agents.

c) Helping to define a marketing plan for the agency so that it can effectively carry out its business.

Companies should also take it upon themselves to see that their agents are successful in carrying out their marketing plans, as the failure of an agency undoubtedly means failure to the insurance company – through unobtained sales. Thus, close and well-established contacts between insurance companies and their agents are necessary for successful marketing.

5) *Association*

This is a fairly recent method of distribution in which preferential terms (e.g. lower rates of premiums or foregoing a medical selection in the case of life insurance, for example, in respect of sums assured below a stipulated amount) for various classes of insurance are offered to members of particular groups. These may be employees of a firm or members of an association or a particular trade or profession. This method aims to gain special access into a large potential market by mass merchandising at low procurement costs. It is undoubtedly effective and has recently been exploited and used more frequently by various insurance companies.

The main advantage of direct channels of distribution or direct-selling systems, as pointed out by Bickelhaupt[6], is that they offer the insurance contract to the policy holder at a lower cost than alternative systems. By cutting out the middlemen, the functions performed are not necessarily eliminated, but the alleged result is the elimination of one or more intermediaries and the performance of their functions on a more efficient and economical basis.

Thus, the adoption of direct channels of distribution, which involves the by-passing of intermediaries, is a major advantage in that the resultant cost savings should be passed on to the consumer in the form of lower premiums.

Indirect Marketing Channels

Indirect channels are systems whereby sales are made to the public through intermediaries. This channel has long been in use and it is still of major importance. The main advantages of indirect channels of distribution to consumers are two-fold – convenience and impartiality.

86

The first advantage of intermediaries is their convenience to the insuring public. Brokers offer a full range of insurance services – motor, life, property, travel and health, etc. – which no single insurance company can provide. They can, therefore, satisfy all the insurance needs of the individual under one roof. Banks and building societies, furthermore, have added insurance to their already broad range of financial services in order to enable customers to conduct virtually all their financial affairs without leaving the building.

The second advantage, that of impartiality, refers to intermediaries which are independent, such as brokers and certain professional agents. By virtue of their independence, they can give impartial advice to consumers concerning the relative merits of a variety of competing insurance brands.

There are three major indirect channels.

1) *Insurance Brokers*
These are independent full time agents whose principal activity is the selling of insurance. (Legally speaking, brokers are buyers of insurance representing policy holders, rather than sellers of insurance on behalf of insurance companies). The main advantage of brokers is that they possess a high level of technical skill and are thus able to offer clients impartial advice, firstly, on the relative merits of different insurance brands and, secondly, on how, if necessary, a client can claim against his policy. By virtue of their close contact with the clients, brokers are able to monitor trends in customer needs and preferences and can feed this information back to insurance companies as marketing intelligence.

There was a tendency towards infiltration of these brokers' roles by individuals who presented themselves as genuine brokers to swindle people caught unawares. Regulatory moves have recently reduced this problem. It was felt that regulation would caution representatives who used techniques such as high-pressure selling which took no account of whether the customer understood (or needed) what was being put before him[40]. Non-regulation could easily have jeopardised the credibility of other genuine intermediaries in the opinion of the public. The Insurance Brokers (Registration) Act, 1977, therefore, prohibited any individual or group of individuals to ascribe himself/ themselves the title of 'insurance broker', 'reinsurance broker', 'assurance broker' or any other title which may infer any of the aforementioned titles unless they are properly registered under the Act.

2) *Part Time "Professional" Agents*

These are individuals or institutions who are not paid by the insurer and whose principal interests lie in their own main field of activity, but who sell insurance to supplement the (professional) services they offer. They include accountants, banks, building societies, estate agents, solicitors and travel agents. They can either be independent agents, offering a range of insurance brands, or exclusive agents, offering the policies of only one insurance company. The professional agency system is a growing practice, especially among the clearing banks who, faced with increasing competition from building societies and savings banks, are seeking to expand and diversify the range of financial services which they offer.

3) *Home Service Agents*

These are individuals, employed by life insurance companies (some on a part time basis), whose primary role is to sell policies and collect premiums from the homes of policy holders. Some part time salespersons are often, however, inadequately trained. The home service agents are often described as a 'direct' channel of distribution, as they are employed by the company. They can either be full time or part time workers. They are mostly found dealing with industrial insurance, which is basically a home service insurance. They give advice to clients and collect premiums from their own homes.

Although both direct and indirect channels of distribution offer advantages to clients in different ways, they have one benefit in common for the insurance company in that they both provide a market feedback function. Among the direct channels of distribution, this function is performed primarily by the company sales representatives. As we saw earlier, sales representatives, by virtue of their close contact with the clients, are able to feed back a continuous supply of marketing information concerning the needs and wants of the market. Equipped with this information, the company can then engage in the development of new products geared to meeting these needs. Similarly, among the indirect channels of distribution, the brokers in particular are able, through their direct dealings with clients, to feed back to the company valuable marketing intelligence concerning trends in consumer needs and preferences.

Channels of Distribution for Life Assurance

In the life assurance industry, the main distribution channels are both direct and indirect ones. Intermediaries, like agents, brokers and banks, are now coming on to the scene. Life policies are also sold directly through company sales forces, mail order and advertisements. Only intermediaries will be considered under this section. (The direct sales force which is very important and expanding, will be dealt with in more detail under the sales force management chapter.)

Historically, the basic intermediary system has been the "agency system", comprising of large networks of full and part time agents, generally linked to one or more companies. Brokers also occupy an influential position in the life assurance industry. The liberal environment in the western world is reflected in a highly developed intermediary system with the brokers playing an important role. Usually, the majority of ordinary life assurance business is obtained through agents, whilst brokers tend to co-ordinate the group business and industrial life assurance handled by industrial agents.

Intermediaries are given considerable promotional and technical support by the life offices, principally in the form of advertising, the provision of technical material, inspectors and other specialist advisers and training courses. The remuneration received by full time agents tends to be through salary or part salary and part commission. Brokers and part time agents are invariably paid by commission, although in some instances the former charge fees, particularly for pension businesses.

An example of an "agency system" office is the Standard Life Assurance Company in Sheffield. The vast majority of this company's business is through agents, usually insurance brokers, but also includes accountants, solicitors, banks and building societies. These agents are only paid commission on business produced. The Standard Life employs representatives, known as Inspectors (the original full title being Inspector of Agencies) whose job is to service these agencies and endeavour to obtain business for the company.

Research has shown that both brokers and agents play an important role in facilitating new product competition and the growth of new life companies by enabling them to establish themselves without the necessity of incurring the expenses of establishing comprehensive branch networks.

Presently, the banks are beginning to emerge as distributors of life assurance. One such bank is the National Westminster Bank Ltd. which has teamed up with Legal and General Assurance Society Ltd. and Friends' Provident Life Office to provide a policy called the National Westminster – Access Life Plan.

The (direct) sales force acts as sales representatives for a particular company. A life assurance salesperson's role has changed in many ways over the years. Just after the war, he was considered as a provider of advice for savings or for retirement and house purchases. He did not require any specialist knowledge or training since most insurance was sold on the basis of endowment assurance over 20 years or to age 65, with an occasional whole life plan with family income benefit[41].

During the 1960's and 1970's a salesperson's task was further complicated by the spate of legislation, tax savings schemes and by inflation. A salesperson had to be knowledgeable in business affairs, law and accountancy in order to advise clients on the best possible deal to suit their needs. Today, the public is buying insurance to provide security as cheaply as possible in the hope that inflation will be contained, but the higher it is, the less credible is the insurance industry's position as either a medium for saving or providing for the future. This makes the sales representative's job more difficult.

At present, great emphasis is placed on marketing life assurances through newspaper advertisements. A considerable amount of business has been generated this way and most companies have built up a large sales force to follow up leads quickly.

The most recent trends in channels of distribution in insurance include:

i) Selling insurance through vending machines. This is suitable for selling standard types of policies (e.g. accident and life assurances in major airports, railway stations, bus stations or supermarkets).

ii) One stop shopping of insurance products. There is a trend towards centralisation and integration of all financial services. In the future, it may well be that all the insurance services and products will be offered in one place (one stop shopping) where other financial services might be also supplied.

Merchandising

Merchandising is a programme aimed at selling insurance policies on a large scale, by offering a certain insurance package at a reduced price. When this package is offered to members of certain groups (e.g. trade associations or professional organisations), it is called mass merchandising because of the large scale of the potential sale. Mass merchandising is used particularly for selling personal insurance (e.g. motor, household and home owners policies).

The premiums charged in a mass merchandising campaign could be up to 20% lower than prices charged to the individual (ordinary) customers. This reduction is possible because of economies of scale in selling and commission.

Whilst the advantages above make mass merchandising attractive to insurance companies, its major disadvantage to the customer lies in the possible disclosure of adverse personal information to other persons (e.g. the employer, trade and professional organisation) who are involved in the implementation of this marketing programme.

The overall objectives of the mass merchandising scheme are:

 i) to obtain a high percentage of individual enrolment; and,

 ii) to reduce acquisition costs and develop continuing administrative systems which enable delivery of the insurance product at a reduced rate.

This concept can be generally divided into three distinct phases:

a) acceptance by the sponsor;

b) the initial solicitation of employees; and,

c) the continuing enrolment of new employees.

This aggressive approach is promoted by the field salesperson, usually with audio-visual aids and careful monitoring of the customer's record and background.

CHAPTER TEN

SALES FORCE MANAGEMENT

Sales force management in insurance involves many diverse and critical functions such as: planning, controlling and directing sales-persons and agents. In addition, it is the responsibility of the sales manager to recruit, train, supervise and motivate insurance sales-persons in their daily functions. The task of an insurance sales force covers a multitude of different job aspects including:

i) locating and meeting prospective insurance buyers;

ii) identifying customers' needs and attitudes;

iii) recommending a product package to fill the needs of the customers;

iv) developing the sales presentation aimed at informing the customer of product attributes and persuading him to buy the recommended package policies;

v) closing the sale; and,

vi) following up to ensure total satisfaction, including paying claims where relevant, thus minimising post-purchase anxiety or cognitive dissonance.

Clearly the selling technique differs from one type of policy or assurance to the next, so it is important to identify the classification in which a salesperson's job falls, and to gear the training to the specific needs of that task.

One of the greatest difficulties of organising sales training programmes is that insurance companies rarely define the *precise* nature of the selling task. However, once the job has been coherently and systematically outlined within a marketing plan, then suitable training of agents and salespersons can be devised.

The sales training programme should relate to:

i) the job description and basic functions;

ii) product knowledge and promotion functions required; and,

iii) the development of contacts.

Generally, the following criticisms of insurance salespersons have been found to be common:

i) They do not know the needs of potential customers.

ii) Their sales approach is poor and they do not sell with conviction and enthusiasm.

The demand for good salespersons is very high, but they are generally hard to find. Personal salesmanship is an integral part of the vast majority of insurance companies as well as of business enterprises generally and the need is definitely for an improvement rather than any curtailment. If each salesperson was better at his job, most insurance companies could have cut back on their sales force.

If so, is training the answer?

Since the problem is basically not to minimise the cost to the company, but to maximise the effectiveness of the sales force, the answer must lie in improved training techniques along with a more selective system of recruitment, coupled with motivation schemes built into the job to ensure that the insurance salesperson gives the job his best at all times.

Due to the competitive nature and difficulties involved in selling insurance, few salespersons are capable of succeeding and the turnover rate is high. It has been found that a turnover rate of 55% in the first year is not uncommon and that these rates are at least 80% within three years[42]. If this high turnover rate is not kept in check, the company will run into serious trouble due to the high costs incurred in the form of salaries and training costs, but most important the vast cost inherent in lost sales, reduced company reputation and permanently burned territory.

To understand the problem of high turnover rates, several areas have to be considered, including:

i) selection;

ii) training; and,

iii) supervision and payment systems.

After considering these in detail, the various bases for evaluating a salesperson's performances will be studied.

Selection

Due to the high turnover rate, recruitment and selection is an important activity in an insurance company. The main sources of recruitment are through personal introduction and through advertisements and agencies. In order to ensure that those recruited will be successful, the selection procedure has to be very thorough. Unfortunately, in spite of the considerable benefits that can accrue to managers through effective recruitment, some of them do not place much importance on selection techniques. Guides to the selection and training of salespersons are available in this industry and should be used more widely.

The advertising for prospective candidates should be done through radio, newspapers and magazines, etc. Typical agents are 25-40 years old, married with children, fairly highly educated and have some selling experience. There is a tendency now to employ more women in selling insurance (particularly life assurances). The typical woman insurance agent is single, divorced or widowed and in certain countries (e.g. Japan) up to 50% of all the life assurance agents are women. They work either full or part time and generally they are highly educated and very diligent. According to Greenberg[42], a clinical psychologist, the traditional criteria for selection, like experience, education, age, race, sex and I.Q., do not determine whether a person has the ability to sell. Rather two personality qualities, ego-drive and empathy, are the factors which make a salesperson successful.

Ego-drive is the need of an individual to make a sale to another for personal gratification rather than monetary reward. The ego-driven individual's self-esteem is enhanced by victories and his determination to succeed is stimulated by failures[43]. Ego-drive is not ambition, aggression or even willingness to work hard, but the satisfaction of success.

Empathy, on the other hand, is the ability to sense accurately the reactions of others and to feel as they do in order to relate effectively to them. This enhances a salesman's ability to get powerful feedback and enables him to adjust his own behaviour to complement his client's behaviour in order to assist him in selling the policy.

Other personality dynamics that are required of a salesperson are:

i) Technical proficiency — he must be conversant with all current legislation pertaining to his trade, be knowledgeable in basic business practice, laws and accountancy so far as it is relevant to insurance and have some ability in investment.

ii) Decision making — the ability to make quick decisions which combine thoughtfulness, responsibility and the courage to act, even to risk, with the intelligence and flexibility to make generally sound judgments and to learn from any mistake which might be made.

iii) Communication — the ability to convey one's ideas, knowledge and skills to others.

iv) Leadership — the ability to get others to do willingly what they have the ability to do, but might not spontaneously do on their own.

v) Delegation — the willingness to allow others to do a job, combined with a capacity to assess accurately their ability to do so.

To aid the selection of potentially successful salespersons, a test has been designed[44] called the *multiple personal inventory* (or MPI test), which takes into account all the above mentioned factors. This test can be used for potential applicants or within the organisation to weed out the less productive members so that the money spent on them can be used for training the successful members instead. Companies like World Service Life and First American Insurance Company have used this test with success.

In daily work routine, the major differences between successful and unsuccessful insurance salespersons are that the former show more of the following behaviour:[45]

i) Allocate specific periods for *work planning*.

ii) Make more *appointments* for seeing prospective clients, using *referred leads*.

iii) Need to contact *fewer* prospects to make a sale and have a *lower percentage* of rejections.

iv) Time spent working in general and time spent in face to face contacts with prospects (in particular) is longer.

Consequently, the criteria for the selection of insurance salespersons should refer to and include qualities such as intitiative and self-discipline, persistence, adaptability, ability to plan, friendliness and consideration, empathy, ego-drive, ability to carry and assume respon-sibilities, to communicate with prospective customers and make decisions, all coupled with suitable aggressiveness.

To sum up, in most insurance marketing situations four characteristics affect the work of a salesperson and his effectiveness: human relations skills, diagnostic skills, selling background and organising ability.

Selling skills have always been regarded as important by companies concerned with insurance marketing. There is an increasing awareness of the value of the skills of understanding and dealing with people which leads to efficient, economical and successful selling. Diagnostic skill is the ability of the agent to assist the customer in identifying and analysing his problems, so that suitable insurance products may be recommended.

Often, many sales orientated insurance companies fail to realise that the individual salesperson is just *one* important factor in the marketing mix. They concentrate on this one element, ignoring or neglecting the other variables which affect the achievements of the insurance company's objectives. Moreover, the effectiveness of a sales force not only depends on its size, but also on how it is organised. This will usually be based on the company's marketing strategy. Basically, there are three types of insurance sales force structures:

i) *Territorial-structured* in which a salesperson is responsible for selling all the insurance company's products in a clearly defined territory.

ii) *Product-structured* (e.g. life, general or industrial) in which a salesperson sells only a few specific products. This specialisation of the sales force by products is effective when the products are rather complex, or where there is such a variety of unrelated insurance products that it becomes quite impossible for a salesperson to deal with all of them.

iii) *Customer-structured* in which different types of sales forces are created to serve the different types of customer. These customers may be the very large companies, industries or government ministries, etc.

Training

A newly recruited salesperson will first attend an intensive course normally lasting for three weeks to familiarise him with the basics of insurance and selling. However, most training is found to be too technically orientated and does not provide sufficient opportunities to practise skills. Furthermore, there are hardly any follow up training courses, except for the theoretical courses and exams that are required for promotion. Thus, the sales representative is left to develop his own skills. This means that a particular salesperson must have exceptional sales ability and self-confidence in order to surmount the initial difficulties. Although the final responsibility for training rests with the branch manager, one reason why these representatives do not receive more on-the-job training is because the manager is more involved in recruiting and selling, since these are more profitable[36].

Finally, the lack of supervision and the great pressures on a representative to succeed can occasionally result in undesirable sales practices, distortion of sales records and other malpractices that are difficult to detect.

All training programmes agree that learning is the key to better performance and Robert W. Bieber[37] suggests the following axioms to guide any would-be trainer:

i) The learner must be the focal point of the training.

ii) If the learner is confronted with a problem he will learn more.

iii) Involvement on the part of the learner is imperative.

iv) Learning is behaviour modified by experience.

However, the basic retention principles must also be borne in mind when selecting a method of teaching (i.e. that you retain 10% of what you read, 20% of what you see, 30% of what you hear, 60% of what you hear and see, 70% of what you talk about and 90% of what you do).

Whatever the principles used, the insurance company training officer must recognise the importance of follow-through training to ensure that the information has been absorbed (repeat reinforcement technique), to provide the salesperson with new insurance products information and keep him informed of new techniques in selling. Total commitment from the learner is also of paramount importance. In order to ensure participation, a relaxed atmosphere is usually recommended as well as the use of small groups, although this differs from one company to another. The approach to the session must be geared to the needs of the salesperson in order to maximise commitment.

The essence of an effective sales training programme is to help a salesperson to know how he/she reacts and how others might react. The training must be tailored to the trainee's needs, personality and attitudes, yet all too often courses are of such a general nature that their real needs are rarely catered for adequately. For example, if the salespersons are old and experienced, it is advisable to stress their professionalism which will, in turn, rekindle their interest in being real professionals. For the young trainee, however, encouragement and confidence-building are the order of the day.

Sales forces selling insurance should also be trained in the principles underlying the company's pricing policy, or indeed its marketing strategy. They should also be trained to know more about the thinking behind his company advertising campaigns (i.e. what promotion material is needed and which one is more effective). In order to be more effective in distribution and selling, sales forces should be trained to understand and appreciate customers' problems and plans and how to make the most from customers' changing personal circumstances.

Supervision and the Payment System

Supervision varies in quantity and quality from manager to manager. It also depends on the ability of the salespersons. The more capable ones are usually left on their own. Normally, little supervision is given after the first three months, but initially, an inexperienced salesman is required to formulate a weekly plan in discussion with his manager. This usually involves target numbers for interviews and contracts to be made during the following week.

Little supervision is found in the field, as managers are generally reluctant to accompany sales representatives on sales calls. Besides, most representatives prefer to work alone and without any direct supervision. Consequently, managers are often ignorant of a representative's particular strengths and weaknesses. Consequently, often the only form of supervision that is in existence after the first three months is the weekly or monthly meetings where sales analysis sheets are completed by the representatives. In some ways, the sales representative is self-employed. However, on the other hand, he is also responsible to a manager. This places both of them in an ambiguous situation and makes supervision considerably more difficult.

In addition, there is hardly any formal training for managers and their selection is not based on their supervision ability, but rather on sales and recruitment records. This contributes to the relative lax supervision system in existence. However, there are some major methods of supervising salespersons in insurance which may prove of use.

1) *Call Norms*

Developing and supervising certain "call norms" (i.e. the number of calls the salesperson must make per week and/or the length of each call). The success of this type of control and supervision depends on a correct assessment of sales response to the number of calls. Some quantitative methods of optimising the 'call times number' have been developed in manufacturing industry that can also be employed in the insurance industry. These mainly involve regression analysis[48] and operational research[49] techniques. While call norms are desirable for particular types of accounts and 'average' types of salespersons, they should be referred to merely as guidelines rather than as requirements. This can be done through optimum use of sales time[50].

2) *Customer Types and Policy Type Group Norms*

Instead of allocating sales effort either by customer types or by product line, the two are combined. Each agent is confronted with a two dimensional grid which he completes:

Table 8
Optimising Sales Time Allocation by Considering Both Customer Type and Product Group(s)

| Customer | Percentage of Sales Effort | | | | Total |
| | Insurance Policies (Products) | | | | |
	1	2	3	4	
A	4.5	13.5	22.5	4.5	45.0
B	3.0	9.0	15.0	3.0	30.0
C	2.5	7.5	12.5	2.5	25.0
Total	10.0	30.0	50.0	10.0	100.0

When confronted with a grid similar to table 8, a salesperson will probably allocate his sales time, based on the highest profit he could bring in and on the most profitable product. In this example, product 3 and customer A seem to be the most productive, so the salesperson should allocate the greatest proportion of his sales time to product 3. He goes on filling up the grid, subject to the percentage of sales calls by product and the percentage of calls by customers. This method is, of course, of importance mainly to salespersons selling general insurance products to large customers.

The method 'forces' the salesperson, when filling in the grid, to consider seriously his chances of selling to the various customers. Instead of allocating sales time by 'feeling' and intuition, it provides a target, or some sort of plan to carry out his sales effort. This method also takes into account the changing market environment (i.e. that certain customers will not increase their insurance/assurance package any further in the future and that certain customers will buy a larger package if the number of calls increases further). Every time the whole procedure is repeated, the salesperson has to think whether customers will change their orders for the coming period and, based on previous experience, the salesperson will be able to forecast their buying patterns relatively accurately.

3) *Supervision for New Accounts*

The identification between active and prospective calls is very important. If left alone, many salespersons tend to spend most of their time dealing with present customers. Present customers are better-known quantities and can be depended upon for some business, whereas a prospect may never deliver any business or deliver it only after many months of effort. Unless the salesperson receives a bonus for *new* customers, he assumes the risks during the "courting" period.

In addition to the problem of how much time is spent in cultivating prospects, there is the problem of which prospect to cultivate. This problem is especially acute in situations where there are more prospects than time available for developing them. Somehow they must be ranked and insurance salespersons should concentrate on the prospects at the top of the list. This can be done by working out a value for the Return On Time Invested (ROTI) for each prospect (see next section).

Salespersons are usually paid a basic salary and a commission based on successful sales of policies. This creates incentives. However, a less competent salesperson will find the job very risky and insecure, since the company provides office facilities but not necessarily financial assistance for the purchase and running of a car and other expenses. The commission based system also means that a good income can be attained by an experienced representative from his commission on existing policies. Consequently, they do not make much effort to bring in new business.

This type of remuneration package has both fixed and variable components. The fixed form of payment can have three ingredients:

i) basic (or basis) payment;

ii) payment according to agent's qualification; and,

iii) allowance for standard sale.

Variable payments (or commission) can be related to:

i) production (i.e. number of sales);

ii) first time premium collected;

iii) premium collection, in general; and,

iv) renewal commission.

A district sales manager in insurance supervises, on average, 15 to 20 salespersons in addition to training new recruits. In addition, there are also regional sales managers who are involved in training (in consultation with district sales managers) and who co-ordinate and administer development programmes of how product, new lines and advertising campaigns should be conducted.

Characteristics and Requirements for High Selling Performance

A clear understanding of the functions of insurance salespersons cannot be over-emphasised. A thorough knowledge of these functions enhances the selection, recruitment, training, supervision and control of the salespersons. Meidan[51] observed that in allocating personal selling effort, failure to define the salesperson's role adequately could lead to poor performance since the salesperson may not even know their tasks and responsibilities exactly. The job of the insurance salesperson also has both strategic and innovative dimensions, just as does that of the sales force management. Many insurance salespersons are faced in their territories with the problems of goal determination, planning and long-term market development. Their work can, therefore, be divided into two broad categories:

i) agency development; and,

ii) sales maintenance.

Both should lead to the generation of additional sales of insurance policies.

1) *Sales Development*

This involves the creation of customers out of people who are either unaware of the insurer's product or those who are simply not interested in the insurance company's products, or even those who are resistant to change. The task requires the reshaping (in some cases) of the prospective buyers' attitudes, habits and patterns of thought. It is a highly creative task which requires considerable time, talents, resourcefulness and ingenuity.

It involves the identification of both possible and probable insurance customers and their needs. By informing and influencing them, the salespersons should be able to create a situation in which each prospective customer should learn for himself that he has needs and problems, thereby arousing the intention and conviction for change.

Finally, the salesperson should stabilise the change created.

2) *Sales Maintenance*

This is primarily the creation of additional sales from existing customers. The objective is the preservation and building of the confidence and acceptance established in the development process. The selling strategy here is defensive rather than offensive. The tactic is to make the insurer's own position entrenched, secure and impregnable to competitors. The main task of the "maintenance salesperson" is to keep the customers content with, and happy in, their relationship with the insurance company.

In both developmental and maintenance selling, insurance salespersons also act as a source of information to the company for their overall market activities. This information concerns the customers, products, competitors and buyer behaviour, etc. and serves as a useful input into the corporate planning process of the company. The way sales forces are organised affects the quantity and quality of the intelligence feedback generated to the insurer. Limited opportunities for intelligence reporting are available under the traditional geographical and product allocation of duties to insurance salespersons and many insurance directors advocate the use of "new accounts" sales forces and "pioneer" sales forces. These give greater scope to ask more questions about the needs of prospects at the time of calls. The questions are vital for the salesperson's own use, while the answers are valuable to the company's future plans. The information generated by the insurance salespersons should be used in further product development, sales forecasting, pricing decisions, analysis of competitors' strategic moves and quantification of any threats from new entrants.

As a result of the special needs of development and maintenance selling, it is often argued that many of the qualities required for successful development selling cannot be acquired. Training can only develop and strengthen the qualities if they are already there, but training cannot enable a person to develop a new and different personality or character traits. As mentioned before there are two critical characteristics for a successful salesperson: empathy and ego-drive.

Empathy was defined as the important central ability to feel as the other fellow does, so as to be able to sell him the product or service. Meyer and Greenberg[52] noted that the salesperson with good empathy serves the reactions of the customer and is able to adjust to those reactions. He is not simply bound by a prepared sales track, but he functions in terms of the real interaction between himself and the customer. Sensing what the customer is feeling, the salesperson is able to change pace, double back on his track and make whatever creative modifications that might be necessary to home in on the target and close the sale.

Ego drive is seen as a particular quality which makes the salesperson want and need to make a sale in a personal or ego way, not merely for the money to be gained. Hence, to the top salesperson the sale provides a powerful means of enhancing his ego. Conversely, failure tends to diminish this ego, although a top salesperson's ego should not be so weak that the "poor self picture" continues for a long time. Rather, failure should act as a stimulus, which with subsequent success, brings ego enhancement. As stated by Meyer and Greenberg[52] *"The salesperson's empathy, coupled with his intense ego drive, enables him to home in on the target effectively and make the sale."*

In the selection of salepersons, it has been observed that experience is less important than a possession of these two central characteristics of empathy and ego drive which are essential for successful selling. Training succeeds when these two raw materials are present. Wilson[53] observed that the performance of a salesperson depends on:

i)   the innate character traits;

ii) training; and,

iii) motivation.

He suggested that selection should be geared towards choosing men and women whose inborn characteristics are suited to the job and who can then be developed and motivated.

In selling insurance policies (particularly life assurances), face to face contact between the salesperson and the potential customer is paramount, because:

i)   insurance customers are heterogeneous, requiring individual attention and service, which consists of fitting a policy that suits the customer's individual characteristics (e.g. age, income, marital status and life style, etc.); and,

ii) the insurance salesperson has to seek out (i.e. *sell*) the policy.

There are a number of approaches to classifying the determinants associated with a salesperson's high selling performance. Among the most important approaches are:

i)   Hughe's "Personality Needs" approach;

ii) SOOT (Self-Other Orientation Tasks) test; and,

iii) biographical variables (table 9).

The "personality needs" approach is based on four characteristics associated with high insurance selling performance: dominance, gregrariousness, altruism and status. The SOOT test suggests that factors such as self-esteem, social interest, self centrality, openness of personality and complexity (as explained in the middle column of the table) are associated with high selling performance. The third approach is based on biographical aspects. Chi square studies[55] have suggested that biographical variables such as education, previous insurance experience, present company experience and personal high income are positively (and significantly) associated with high selling performance. Other biographical factors (e.g. age, gender, marital status and persistency) were found to be not significantly related to sales performance. Other studies[57] have found positive correlations between a salesperson's job performance, their motivation, and their belief in their products.

Spear[56] suggests that, whilst there are no significant differences between the mental ability test scores of successful vs. unsuccessful salespersons, there are a number of personality traits that characterise successful insurance salespersons:

i)   not moody or subject to worry;

Table 9

Determinants of Success for Insurance Agents

Some Major Approaches

Personality "Needs" Approach[54]	SOOT TEST or Self-Other Orientations Tasks[56]	Biographical Variables
1. *Dominance* (i.e. need to dominate and convince others)	1. *Self esteem*	1. Previous insurance experience
2. *Gregarious* (i.e. the need of meeting with people)	2. *Social interest* (i.e. showing concern for others)	2. Present company experience
3. *Altruism* (i.e. satisfaction in listening to other people's problems)	3. *Self centrality*	3. Personal income
4. *Status* (i.e. desire for success and/or security)	4. *Openness* (i.e. seeking acceptance and association with others)	4. Education
	5. *Complexity* (i.e. the number of words/aspects that a salesperson can use to describe his work and personality)	

  ii) self confidence;

 iii) aggressiveness;

 iv) willingness to assume responsibility;

  v) sociable;

 vi) not resentful of criticism; and,

vii) unconventional.

The following *self-reporting* personality traits are also considered to be associated with success in selling insurance policies:

  i) emotional stability;

 ii) aggressiveness;

iii) extroversion;

iv) self-sufficiency; and,

 v) sociability.

The performance of the insurance salesperson depends also on the quality of supervision. In this context, earlier research[57] has indicated that the most important supervisor's characteristics are:

  i) supervisor's rank;

 ii) supervisor's experience;

iii) his age and age differential (to that of the supervised);

iv) age of the territory (agency);

 v) salesperson's experience; and,

vi) supervisor's prior management experience.

The criteria for assessing a salesperson's success by these supervisors are:

  i) the total value of policies sold per annum;

 ii) net paid premiums paid on policies sold;

iii) new business policies sold; and,

iv) renewal policies sold.

Obviously, situational characteristics (e.g. th company characteristics, agency history and external organisational ors) are also of major importance. Certain insurance companies accept a high turnover — up to 90% of new salespersons are not with the same company within a four year timespan. Their argument is that agents who leave the company are the unsuccessful ones, so a higher turnover leads to increased turnover and the maximisation of *net* sales revenues.

In order to be successful in selling insurance, the salesperson has to be aware of the four major stages or phases, as indicated in figure 12. The first stage refers to identification of potential customers from a number of sources (e.g. call-ins, referrals, advertising response or centres of influence). As soon as a distinctive potential prospect has been identified (stage II), the main question is: who is (are) the decision maker(s)? This is necessary in order to be able to focus selling efforts on the potential decision maker(s) and to follow this up later by a call and an offer of an acceptable insurance product. The acceptance of the offered insurance product is a function of the sensitivity to the policy price (premium) and the buyer's attitudes towards risk and uncertainty. The final stage is the sale which includes undersignment of the client, payment of the first premium and policy delivery.

Bases for Evaluating Sales Force Performance

Unlike many jobs in which quantitative measures of effectiveness are difficult or impossible to develop (i.e. where there is an over-reliance on subjective and qualitative judgments), the insurance salesperson's job permits certain objective, quasi-quantitative performance measures to be employed. Since the insurance selling job is multidimensional, both the descriptive and quantitative methods are best used in combination, in order to appraise the overall job of selling performed by individual salespersons (table 10).

The most common objective measure is also the simplest: insurance sales volume produced (i.e. the insurance salesperson who consist-ently makes the most sales is the best one). However, this yardstick alone is seldom a sufficient measure in situations when insurance salespeople are expected to find their own customers without territorial restraint. Almost all the other methods taken on their own have their deficiency and limitations. For example, call rate is a measure of the number of calls made per week, *not* necessarily of effectiveness. Similarly, the average number of policies sold per work day tells very little about the sales volume of these policies.

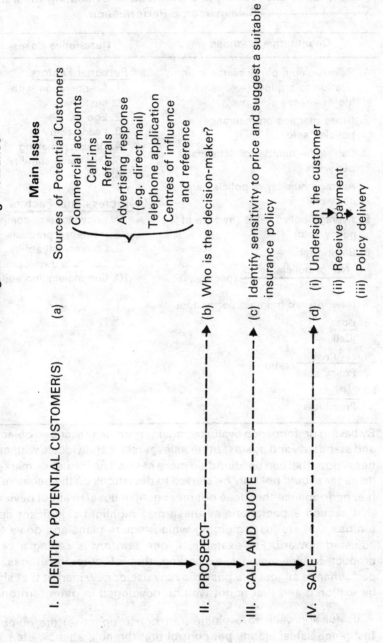

Figure 12
The Four Main Distinctive Stages in Selling Insurance

Main Issues

I. IDENTIFY POTENTIAL CUSTOMER(S) (a) Sources of Potential Customers
- Commercial accounts
- Call-ins
- Referrals
- Advertising response (e.g. direct mail)
- Telephone application
- Centres of influence and reference

II. PROSPECT (b) Who is the decision-maker?

III. CALL AND QUOTE (c) Identify sensitivity to price and suggest a suitable insurance policy

IV. SALE (d) (i) Undersign the customer
(ii) Receive payment
(iii) Policy delivery

Table 10
Quantitative and Descriptive Methods of Evaluating Insurance Salesperson's Performance

Quantitative Methods	Descriptive Bases

1. Sales volume performance or in relation to a quota (e.g. value of life assurance sold p.a.)	a) Personal Factors
	   1. Co-operation with customers
	   2. Ego-drive
	   3. Leadership

2. Gross margins on insurance policies sold	4. Decision making
	   5. Emotional stability
	   6. Empathy

3. Call rate – number of calls made per week	
4. Average number of policies sold per week	b) Professional Factors 7. Knowledge of company insurance products
5. Average policy value (by type of policy sold)	8. Commercial ability 9. Contacts development
6. Batting ratio $= \dfrac{\text{No. of policies sold}}{\text{calls made}}$ (per week)	10. Communication abilities
7. New insured (number per period)	
8. $\dfrac{\text{Cost}}{\text{Call}}$ ratio	
9. $\dfrac{\text{Cost}}{\text{Policy sold}}$ ratio	
10. $\dfrac{\text{Profits}}{\text{Premiums}}$ ratio	

By having performance evaluated against certain prescribed objectives and standards and against other salespersons, individuals with managerial potential can be identified more easily. The insurance marketing manager should not only be alerted to deviations on the negative side (i.e. performance that does not meet goals), but also about deviations that exceed expectations as these may highlight significant opportunities that are just emerging which require plans and goals to be adjusted upward. For example, if one territory is selling a certain product in volumes far exceeding that of other territories, this performance suggests a possible new use or new market that should be explored and that might well be developed in other territories.

A useful approach to evaluate (but not to optimise) the number of insurance salespersons per control unit (branch, agency, etc.), is by evaluating how much time should be spent on each customer. This can be done by working out a value for the Return On Time Invested (ROTI) for each account. ROTI was first presented by Cravens, Woodruff and Stamper[58] and discussed with relation to possible practical applications in the marketing of products by Vizza[59]. The first step in ROTI is to find the value of an insurance salesperson's time — the usual unit used is the hour. There are two methods of calculating this, on a cost basis and on a break-even sales volume basis. The second approach, which is more useful for account classification, is the break-even sales volume; that is the insurance sales volume that must be produced to cover costs. In order to calculate break-even sales volume, the gross margin on sales must be known. Thus the break-even volume, equals direct costs divided by the percentage of gross margin on sales, hence the break-even volume per hour equals direct costs divided by the gross margin percentage. This tells the salesperson how much he must sell per hour to cover his costs. Finally, the return on time invested can be obtained from the gross margin divided by the cost of time invested. A ROTI value greater than one is profitable, while less than one is unprofitable.

Thus, by calculating ROTI values for accounts, they can be systematically classified into Grade A, — high ROTI value; Grade B, — medium ROTI value; Grade C, — low ROTI value, with the insurance salesperson's time being allocated accordingly.

To summarise in symbols:

$$CPCH = \frac{DC}{CH}; \quad BEV = \frac{DC}{GMP}; \quad ROTI = \frac{GM}{CTI}; \quad BEV/CHr = \frac{CPCH}{GMP}$$

ROTI > 1 Profitable, ROTI < 1 Unprofitable.

where CPCH   = Cost per call hour
       DC   = Direct costs
       CH   = Call hours
       BEV   = Break-even volume
       BEV/CHr = Break-even volume per call hour
       GMP   = Gross margin percentage
       GM   = Gross margin cash on sales obtained
       CTI   = Cost of time invested
       ROTI   = Return on time invested

On this basis, the number of insurance salespersons per control unit and the number of potential customers per insurance salesperson can be allocated. ROTI, however, treats the selling function as a routine job and is *not*, therefore, suitable for optimising the number of sales-persons engaged, for example, in selling insurance and developing a new market territory.

A salesperson's index performance has been developed for assessing composite sales performance for goods marketing[60]. This index can be applied — with some alterations — to assessing an insurance sales-person's performance, as presented in table 11. Some additional methods for assessing salesperson's performance are presented by Meidan[51].

Insurers' selling performance has recently received increasing attention in literature[67]. At the same time, the prospects of selling insurance through 'new' distribution channels[62] and to 'new' customers[68] is under investigation by many insurance companies. This is achieved mainly through product innovation[64] and suitable pricing policies[65].

Table 11
**Insurance Salesperson's Performance Index ** **

Performance Measures (per week)	1 Performance Attained	2 Performance Standard (or quota)	3 Performance Attained (1:2) x 100	4 Weight Assigned	5 Weighted Index of Performance Attainment (4 x 3)
a) Sales policies revenue (£ '000)	461.0	500.0	92.2	0.7	64.5
b) Policies sold (units)	96	100	96	0.8	76.8
c) New customers	48	36	133.3	1.5	200.0
d) Prospect meetings	192.0	160.0	120.0	1.6	192.0
e) No. of calls*	92	75	122.7	1.3	159.5
Totals				5.9	692.8
Composite sales-persons' performance index (total of 5: total of 4)					117.4

* Other factors after e) can be included depending on situation

** Based on Adkins[60]

CHAPTER ELEVEN

MARKETING STRATEGIES IN INSURANCE

The literal meaning of the word *strategy* is *"the art of the general"*, deriving from the ancient Greek word for general, 'strategos'. In fact, the usage of the word dates back to at least 400 B.C., but did not appear in writings until the late eighteenth century. Prior to Napoleon's times, the word had a military connotation implying the art and science of directing military forces to defeat an enemy or to mitigate the results of defeat. Although deriving from an ancient heritage, the term strategy has found its way into management literature in the past decade or so. To insurance people, the term strategy has come to mean the type of decision made by top insurance managers concerning the relationship between the insurance organisation and its environment. In other words, strategy describes those critical boundary-spanning decisions that define the framework and direction for overall marketing organisation management.

We are now in a position to re-define an insurance marketing strategy, although such a definition does not lend itself to a simple sentence. Rather it entails the following:

i) Identifying the market target and its needs.

ii) Planning on the marketing objectives and mix to appeal to this target group with due regard to internal circumstances.

iii) Attention to external forces.

An insurance company's strategy is a plan for action that determines how an insurance company can best achieve its goals and objectives in the light of the existing pressures exerted by competition, on the one hand, and its limited resources, on the other hand. The principal sub-activities in formulating a strategy are:

i) Identifying opportunities and threats to the insurance company's environment.

ii) Estimates of the risks of various alternatives.

iii) Appraising the insurance company strengths and weaknesses.

iv) Matching iii) to i) above, while considering ii).

There are two broad categories of marketing strategies: growth strategies and competitive marketing strategies, as elaborated below. The marketing strategy as applicable to the insurance industry may be summarised in table 12.

Table 12
Marketing Strategies in Insurance

Stages	Examples/Elaboration
Identification of target market(s)	Segmentation by customers' occupations risks and hazards, social class, geographical position, etc.
Marketing objective(s)	Satisfaction of customers' needs Sales revenue Profit Risk spreading Department performances
Marketing mix:	
a) Product	e.g. Types of standards of services, variety of products offered
b) Place (distribution)	e.g. Direct channels of distribution, indirect channels of distribution, salespersons, etc.
c) Promotion (advertising)	e.g. Advertising in appropriate media, promotional literature, insurance company image
d) Price	e.g. Package deals, special discounts, groups discounts, etc.
External forces (non-controllable by the individual insurance company)	Macro environment: economic, political, social and cultural conditions, governmental, legal and technological forces, competitive situation

Growth Strategies

Whichever strategy an insurance company decides to apply, it is significantly determined by the marketing objectives and the target market. The marketing mix will have to be planned accordingly, whilst external factors will presumably have to be given due attention as well. There are various examples of this category of strategies.

1) *Geographical Expansion*

As the name implies, such a strategy seeks to expand sales by extending the physical frontiers of its activities. In pursuing this course of action, an insurance company will no doubt seriously consider the commercial viability of establishing agencies in new additional locations.

2) *Market Penetration*

The employment of this strategy aims at attracting new customers from existing markets. This is undoubtedly the most popular strategy amongst insurance companies. An insurance company which has identified its market and the market needs and has set formal marketing objectives, should be able to plan the marketing mix in the best possible way. Such a company would be placed in an advantageous position, not least as a result of its organised promotional operations. A well-planned market penetration strategy should also win new customers through its better understanding of their needs, a situation which allows management to work on important matters such as image to emphasise the right segments and prices and to make better sales contacts.

3) *New Market Strategy*

This strategy seeks to widen its appeal to attract customers from segments of the market which the insurance company in the past has not concentrated upon. Such a strategy may either attempt to secure new types of customers in addition to its 'traditional' ones, or it may resolve to replace its past market segment appeal. Such a decision may be taken either because the company wants to tap a potential market or because its past reliance on certain segments has been found not to be totally satisfactory.

Of the marketing mix variables, the most important factors that the insurance company should consider when a new market strategy is adopted, are quite obviously the promotion and product variables. In the case of a company that contemplates "replacing" its market altogether, a thorough plan on the whole of the marketing approach would necessarily have to be thrashed out. However, preceding all that, it may also be necessary and worthwhile for the insurance company to conduct a market research in order to evaluate or to confirm the potential areas of the market.

4) *Strategy for Cutting Costs*

One of the questions which any insurance company manager must continually ask himself is "How can cost-efficient operations be obtained so that profitability can be increased?" Manufacturing companies can improve operations by leverage (e.g. by purchasing faster and more reliable machinery), but most service industries, including insurance, are not able to follow this approach. Nevertheless, there is a misconception about service businesses not being able to obtain operating leverage. Operating leverage potential exists in any business organisation as long as a change in operations would result in a drop in the relative cost per unit of output. Substitution of capital for labour is the classic method of obtaining such leverage in both product and service-orientated businesses. Capital is used to purchase machinery (e.g. a computer for an insurance company) which can produce and sell a product at a faster rate with more consistent service. Many insurance companies use the same basic technique, but in different ways. The sales task is broken into its component parts of initial contact, presentation and closing the deal, as well as the different people who perform each function. In each case, the service is further broken down and the aspects that can be performed by less expensive labour are identified. The expensive labour is then free to do those crucial tasks that bring profits to the insurance company.

The strategies for growth require information and decision making in questions such as:

i) From what sources does the insurance company expect to acquire the additional volume growth? Usually, the answer lies in a market research study that investigates potential customers' behaviour, territories and buying preferences, etc.

ii) What is the anticipated rate of growth (i.e. what is, or will be, the company's future market share by sales area(s) and principal lines of coverage)? This again can be obtained through a forecasting study that should be based on information provided by the marketing research department.

iii) What changes in the sales force (agents and company personnel) will be necessary? This information can be supplied by the planning department in conjunction with the training and sales force management section.

iv) What role will automation play in the future in dealing with issues such as rate making, policy issue, accounting and statistical operations and claims settlement, etc., and what influence will automation have on future costs and profitability?

Competitive Marketing Strategies

Kotler[11] rightly states that a company's marketing strategy depends on many factors, one of which is its size and position in the market. From this assertion, he suggests that one method of classifying marketing strategies is to place the company in accordance with its competitive position; namely, as to whether it is a market leader, a challenger, a follower or a 'nicher'. In effect, these are behavioural strategies ordered in relation to the company's market share.

It appears that this idea may be suitably adapted to our concern with insurance marketing, though the author does not fully agree with Kotler's method of labelling *per se*, because it is felt that an insurance company's marketing strategy need not wholly be dictated by its market share. For instance, a small insurance company may still adopt an aggressive market-challenger-type of strategy. Hence, strict correlation between the name of the strategy (i.e. market leader to market nicher) and the market share, should perhaps not be made.

There are four competitive marketing strategies.

1) *Market-Leader Strategy*
This strategy can only be employed by very large, dominant insurance companies. In addition to having a strong distribution network, as they are large they enjoy the benefits accruable from economies of scale. These in turn allow them either to protect their market share or to expand and become even more dominant.

These dominant insurance companies have an influential role in the industry by the virtue of their size. Their promotional activities, based on a well-established reputation, put them in the position as "guardians" of the industry, particularly on prices and promotional intensities.

2) *Market-Challenger Strategy*
This strategy is characterised by the aggressiveness of the marketing tactics. Typically, insurance companies which follow this strategy are those which are ambitiously trying to grow as fast as they can. They tend to be innovative and opportunistic in their marketing approach and are sensitive to changes and developments in their market and in the trade.

3) *Market-Follower Strategy*

Some insurance companies prefer to adopt more cautious tactics. Rather than be aggressive and attract the attention of the leading companies, they choose to settle for a role of following the leaders. Other companies may follow simply because they are not in a position to behave otherwise. Yet others pursue this strategy, but do so with carefully planned paths in order to achieve their long-term targets. In general, market followers possess strong management who give priority to profitability, rather than the market share of their insurance company.

4) *Market-Nicher Strategy*

As the name suggests, such a strategy aims to take advantage of the niches that exist in the market. This is done through specialisation. The markets here are relatively small and tend to go beyond the interests of the large companies, but to the smaller insurance company they are safe and profitable.

Every insurance company must consider how it can build and protect a strong competitive position. At any point in time, the enterprise must recognise that its "strategic posture" depends partly on the competitive environment. Service businesses often require different competitive strategies from those of product-orientated commodities. If an enduring insurance institution is to be created, some attention must be given to the management of economies of scale, proprietary technology, and the reputation of the company. These "barriers" are not just defensive moves; they are necessary if an insurance company is to make progress in trying to achieve its goals.

The selection of an appropriate strategy is based on a careful marketing strategy plan (figure 13). The appraisal by an insurance company of alternative strategies is based on the internal conditions and external forces facing it. These alternative strategies should then be evaluated by the board of directors or the company's business policy team and a selected 'optimum' marketing strategy recommended. If accepted, this recommendation should be carried forward and adequate plans made which involve mainly the determination of means (i.e. allocation of resources) to achieve those objectives. It is the responsibility of the board to implement the plan(s) and to monitor their achievements.

Figure 13
Insurance Marketing Strategy Plan

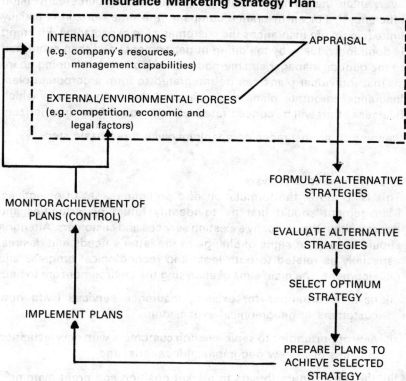

Insurance Corporate Planning and Marketing

Formal insurance corporate planning is particularly essential in the current economic climate in order that insurance companies can realistically consider their use of resources. In addition, an efficient corporate plan is an important tool for decision making throughout the whole organisation.

Corporate planning attempts to integrate two organisational approaches – 'bottom up' and 'top down'. If the approach is *all* 'bottom up' then strategy formulation becomes very difficult. Conversely, if it is *all* 'top down', there is often lack of realism in the plans and a lack of commitment to the plans by the employees in that company[66].

Before plans are made, a time horizon has to be fixed. This is the period over which the company seeks to optimise its resource-conversion efficiency[67]. For an insurance company, the time horizon is usually finite (e.g. in life insurances the customer's life expectancy). Planning is done individually by the different departments and then submitted to the general manager and members of the corporate planning board so that individual plans can be integrated to form a corporate plan. Insurance corporate plans evolve around the main areas in which business effort will be concentrated over the span of the time horizon.

Planning in an insurance company involves three basic steps.

1) *Environmental Analysis*
This is to aid in the formulation of a preliminary set of objectives. Management should first try to identify future opportunities and threats within the company's existing services and customers. Attention should be paid to signs of change in the latter's needs and desires, especially as related to both legal and technological progress and development. The main aims of analysing the environment are to find:

i) new opportunities for existing insurance services (with new customers or geographical expansion);

ii) new opportunities to serve existing customers with new insurance services or in new geographical locations; and,

iii) the major future threats to market position and profit margins[68].

2) *Appraisal of the Company's Resources*
The resources of insurance organisations include manpower, financial strength, market position, management competence and the lowest possible level of susceptibility to external pressures. The purpose of this appraisal is to examine not only the strengths and weaknesses of the existing resources, but also what resources might be available in the future and possible ways in which future resources might be generated. This provides the basis for the planning of future marketing strategy, as explained in the previous pages.

3) *Objectives*
Besides financial objectives, such as stability of profits, risks spread, etc., insurance companies might be interested in increasing their market share, diversification and growth. Whilst some of the objectives may appear of importance in the short term, in the long term, they all ultimately contribute to maximise profitability.

After establishing the objectives and setting a plan of action to achieve them, a thorough appraisal of the new plan is required to evaluate the effectiveness of the proposed actions. Effectiveness is defined as a measure of the fulfilment of an objective, goal, standard or target.

CHAPTER TWELVE

MARKETING ORGANISATION AND CONTROL

Insurance organisations are generally structured around an amalgam of products, functions and locations. We may find in insurance organisations, marine, fire, marketing, and statistics departments and several location points which are serviced by product and function departments. The structure of organisations is basically product orientated, and we must mention that for many insurance companies, especially those in developed market economies, the present structure has been greatly influenced by developments in the field of legislation which created a wall around some insurance products.[69]

Marketing Department Organisation

An efficient marketing organisation structure is really a function of the marketing strategy adopted by the insurance company. Objectives for the insurance marketing department are established in the form of descriptions of the marketing department responsibilities in terms of sales volume, market share, advertising, promotion, product development and market research. This analysis leads to a preliminary estimate of the number of marketing persons required, given the opportunities in the market. The statement of marketing objectives leads also to an estimate of the marketing budget required which must also consider the availability of financial resources and other company constraints.

The next step in the decision process for the insurance marketing manager is to develop the basic control units from which he plans to organise and control the marketing efforts. He must decide the basis for these units (e.g. product, geographic, etc.), as well as the span of control to be used. Using estimates of market potential and expected revenues, the marketing manager must allocate sales effort to the control units. Here, he must consider the individual salesperson's workload, the average number of calls they can perform and how the total sales force should be organised.

Generally, the marketing department is just one of the seven or so major departments in a 'typical' insurance organisation (figure 14). In the past, most of the marketing emphasis in an insurance company was on the sales function, the other major functions and sections in the marketing department were marketing research, advertising, promotion and product planning. This type of marketing department organisation is called *functional organisation*. The advantage of this

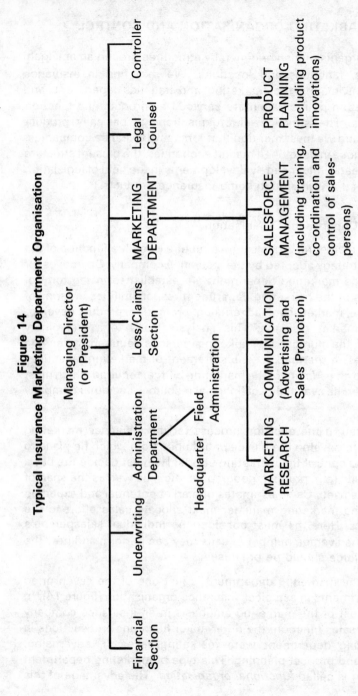

Figure 14
Typical Insurance Marketing Department Organisation

Managing Director (or President)

- Financial Section
- Underwriting
- Administration Department
  - Headquarter
  - Field Administration
- Loss/Claims Section
- MARKETING DEPARTMENT
  - MARKETING RESEARCH
  - COMMUNICATION (Advertising and Sales Promotion)
  - SALESFORCE MANAGEMENT (including training, co-ordination and control of sales-persons)
  - PRODUCT PLANNING (including product innovations)
- Legal Counsel
- Controller

type of organisation is that it leads to a better utilisation of specialist resources in the various functions and is, therefore, a more effective form of organisation. Its limitation is, however, in the ability of the management to control or assess performance in the individual sections (e.g. marketing research). (There is one single function — sales force management — where suitable techniques to control performance have been developed as elaborated in the previous chapters of this book).

The organisation structure of the sales force and its effectiveness depends, however, also on the insurance company's marketing strategy. There are three basic types of marketing structures.

1) *Geographical Organisation*
In this type of organisation, a salesperson can be responsible for selling all the company's policies in a clearly defined territory. The territorially structured (or geographical) organisation is the "traditional" and quite widely used form of insurance sales organisation. In this type of organisation, a salesperson would report either to a regional or a district sales manager. The major benefit of territorial organisation is the lower level of travel time and the economies in operating expenses.

2) *Organisation by Insurance Products*
Product-organised marketing is one in which a salesperson sells only a few specific sets of insurance products (e.g. life assurances, casualty or general insurance). This specialisation of the sales force by products is effective where there is a great variety of unrelated or different policies, so it becomes quite impossible for a salesperson to deal with all of them. The organisation by products is sometimes deemed necessary in selling insurance when customers' needs require specialised technical or environmental risks knowledge.

3) *Organisation by Customers*
A customer-structured sales force is one in which different types of sales forces are created to serve the different types of customers. These customers may be farmers, businessmen, tourists or travellers, etc.

This last type of structure appears more harmonious with the marketing concept and its implication of a customer orientation, as it should lead to a better understanding of the needs and problems of the various insurance customer categories. However, rather surprisingly, it is only very seldom employed in selling insurance.

Insurance Marketing Control

An important factor in insurance marketing is marketing control, whereby an organised feedback system is used to evaluate the performance of insurance marketing strategies. In dynamic market conditions, strategic targets and tactical operations should be under continuous appraisal so that an organisation retains the initiative in its markets.

The control of marketing performance can be by profitability or by turnover (sales volume). For *each* of these two alternative forms of control, the insurance company should check and compare the performance of:

  i)   channels of distribution (agent/insurance salespersons, etc.);

  ii) major markets/territories;

 iii) major products (or groups of products); and,

 iv) individual customers' segments.

The performance should then be compared against the company's targets (or standards), *or* past performance on each of these criteria and/or against the performance of the leading companies in the industry (or the average in the insurance industry, if known).

The same analyses should be performed for the other major type of control, as indicated in figure 15. It should be emphasised that these two forms of control are not alternative to each other, but complementary. While profitability figures might be of interest to insurance company shareholders, owners, very large customers or investors, as an indicator of company's future ability to settle claims, pay large dividends, etc., the turnover ratios relate to the company's strategic posture (i.e. its potential growth and future development in relation to competitive insurance companies). The loss (negative profit) ratios, on the other hand, are mainly indicators of marketing resources efficiency use.

All the eight measures for control are of very great operational importance to the marketing manager in the insurance company. The company will be able to delete or drop certain insurance products that are not profitable enough or with a "too low" sales volume. In addition, the marketing research section will be able to identify problem areas in order to undertake research with a view to finding out

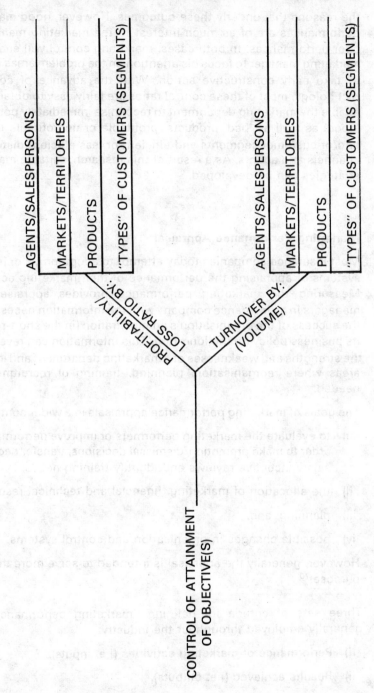

Figure 15
Types of Marketing Control in an Insurance Organisation

the reasons that underly these outcomes. However, good marketing performances are of as much interest to the marketing manager as poor performances. In both cases, marketing control will enable the marketing manager to focus his attention on the problem areas in order to take early constructive action. With the advance of computer technology, most of these control ratios are fairly easy to obtain. They enable the marketing department to recognise immediately potentially 'good' as well as 'bad' products, profitable or unprofitable markets and/or customer segments and efficient or less efficient distribution channels and agents. As a result of this research, suitable marketing strategies can be developed.

Marketing Performance Appraisal

Most insurance companies today attempt to adopt formal or informal systems of appraising the performance of their marketing activities. Measuring the marketing performance provides appraisers and managers in an insurance company with the information necessary for the success of the organisation's administration (in the short-run) and its business policy (in the long-run). This information can reveal both the strengths and weaknesses of a marketing department and indicate areas where reorganisation, planning, training or recruitment are needed.

The goals of marketing performance appraisals in a wider context are:

i) to evaluate the marketing performers or improve performance in order to make promotion/dismissal decisions, transfer decisions, salary incentive reviews and identify training needs;

ii) the allocation of marketing, financial and technical resources;

iii) planning; and,

iv) possible changes in organisation and control systems.

However, generally the appraisal is intended to serve more than one purpose.[70]

Three sets of criteria for defining "marketing performance" are generally employed throughout the industry:

i) Performance of marketing activities (i.e. inputs).

ii) Results achieved (i.e. outputs).

iii) Personal qualities (i.e. personality traits of the marketing sales-person and/or managers assessed).

The second set of criteria (outputs) is most appropriate on the whole, especially for marketeers or salespersons with a higher degree of autonomy and where the decision is to promote/demote/sack. Inputs become more appropriate but results achieved are still important where marketeers have little autonomy, but follow laid down procedures and when counselling, transfer, training needs, decisions and human inventory compilation become important.

Securing an effective measure of outputs is simply a matter of providing units of objective measurement which is probably fairly easy in insurance companies. In addition to the above criteria, there are several other criteria for appraising marketing performance in an insurance company, as elaborated in table 13.

While absolute sales and sales analysis relate to variations from sales plans or quotas, market share analysis compares performance of salespersons with each other or that of competitors. Costs analysis has increased in importance lately because of rapidly rising distribution costs. Accordingly, insurance companies concentrate their attention on sales costs control in order to achieve higher profitability.

The types of costs relevant to sales cost analysis are:

i) *"Natural" costs* — those typically found in accounting records and referring to the nature of expenditure (e.g. telephone or overall car expenses).

ii) *Functional costs* — those which refer to the costs classified by the purpose of the activity (e.g. costs attributable to contacting *particular* customers such as specific travelling costs).

iii) *Direct costs* — those related to insurance sales office expenses.

There are certain problems involved in analysing and allocating sales costs. However, despite the cost and time involved, investigating company's sales performance through a cost analysis approach might lead to an opportunity to identify areas for corrective action (e.g. removal of unprofitable territories, unprofitable customers, unprofitable insurance products or inefficient salespersons)[71].

Table 13

Criteria for Appraising Marketing Performance[70] in an Insurance Company

Key Areas for Assessing Marketing Performance	Ease of Quantification		Objectivity/ Subjectivity	Technique	Typical Quantitative Measures
	Conceptual	Practical			
1. Profitability	Easy	Laborious but routine	Objective but some judgment involved	Routine data collection and analysis	1. Net profit by market/ product (or group of products) 2. Profitability per customer segments 3. Distribution channel/salespersons profitability 4. Expense ratios
2. Market Position	Fairly easy	Laborious but often routine with some ad hoc investigations	Objective (once definitions decided on)	Agents, sales figures Market research	1. Absolute sales and sales analysis 2. Trends 3. Market share 4. Numbers and size of competitors

Table 13 continued

3. Product Leadership	Not easy	Not easy	Mainly judgmental	Internal Executive Panel Market research	1. Ordinal ranking of insurance policies offered with those of competitors 2. Ordinal ranking of value of service range 3. Consumer satisfaction on attitude scales
4. Sales Personnel Performance	Easy	Fairly easy	Mixture of objective data and subjective judgment	Human resource accounting techniques Staff inventory	1. Percentage of appropriately qualified staff at all grades 2. Percentage of promotable salespersons 3. Percentage upgrading of qualifications 4. Percentage ranked "better than average"

CHAPTER THIRTEEN

RECENT DEVELOPMENTS AND FUTURE TRENDS IN INSURANCE MARKETING

The recent rapid changes in the economy generally and in the intensification of competition between insurance companies will have an inevitable effect on the marketing of insurance policies. The most significant recent developments are studied in this final chapter.

Automation

The development of the electronic digital computer has enabled companies to process data and obtain information more rapidly. This greater and more rapid flow of information enables sounder underwriting and better actuarial and investment decisions. In addition, sophisticated investment analysis can be undertaken, while underwriting evaluation of applications can be processed by the computer.

In concrete terms, the computer will enable an insurer to:

i) bill his customers automatically and directly;

ii) identify flat cancellation of policies;

iii) eliminate "red tape"; and,

iv) effect significant economies both in time and costs, allowing lower prices and more effective competition.

Most of the large scale computers in the insurance industry so far have been acquired by life companies or by groups of fire and casualty companies. Direct billing is of particular benefit to motor insurance companies that bill every 3 to 6 months. Automation is obviously also of value for cost accounting, the payroll and general budgetary control of the insurer's expenses. The use of computers has already changed the functions of branches as accounting, underwriting, statistical work, costing, bureau reports and servicing of personal insurance lines are becoming less important functions at branch level.

New Products

Insurance companies regularly place new products on the market, but these new products are now becoming more sensitive to the financial needs of the buyer and less constrained by the existing system of agent/company regulation and computer capabilities.

Investments

The insurance companies have recently started to lend money directly to businesses instead of indirectly through investment bankers or the stock exchange[72]. In this way, they can exert more control over credit and security terms. The active home building industry has also enabled the life assurance companies to transfer their funds from relatively low yield government securities to higher yield mortgages.

Institutional Advertising

In the U.S.A., a considerable amount of advertising is undertaken by the Institute of Insurance or by the Association of Life Assurance Companies, rather than by individual companies. The purpose of this type of advertising is to create public awareness of the advantages of insurance or life assurance and to emphasise the merits of insurance in general rather than the merits of a particular company's products and services. This form of advertising is less costly and benefits everyone. It is beginning to be used in the U.K. as well. Occasionally, advertisements are placed, for example, by The Life Offices' Association and Associated Scottish Life Offices in magazines and newspapers.

Changing Emphasis of Marketing Procedures

With rising inflation, the future will see a change of emphasis towards marketing procedures that can be used effectively as price-conscious buyers force a 'squeezing-down' of sales loads[73]. Most companies are being forced to find ways and means of reducing costs. The number of commission salespersons and individual agency systems will probably be reduced drastically and there will be more emphasis on mass merchandising methods. The reduced sales force will comprise mostly highly trained and technically competent marketing specialists.

The increasing public awareness of the need for insurance, coupled with the wide variety of products needed to suit everyone, is expected to change the public's attitude towards purchasing insurance to a more positive one. At the same time, more emphasis will need to be placed on life cycle client accounts, whereby an individual would be programmed by the salesperson to allocate his risks or financial security money to meet his needs arising from death, disability, sickness, accident, general and property risks. At pre-determined periods, he would be re-programmed to meet life cycle changes, utilising the build-ups in the account. This 'product' will, hopefully, solve all the distributive, consumer and administrative problems facing the insurance industry today.

There is also evidence of a decreasing consumer interest in individual life insurance products for death protection with increasing consumer interest in savings and investment. So, the life assurance companies should concentrate on the latter aspect of their services since they will be facing stiff competition from other financial institutions. It is quite apparent that, in the future, there will be an almost complete disappearance of one-line companies and a trend for the merger of insurance companies with other financial institutions (e.g. merchant banks and joint stock banks) in order to reduce competition and to combat high operational costs. On the basis of recent economic/ marketing developments in the industry, a number of changes and tendencies are expected (figure 16).

1) *Increase in the Importance and the Use of Marketing Research*
In comparison to other industries not much market research has been done on insurance. It is indeed recommended that market research should be more widely used as a tool for identifying:

i) *Consumer Attitudes and Needs*   In the United States it has been found recently that a much lower premium rate is not the major determinant in the purchase of policy. Other factors such as the ability of the salesperson, the reputation of the company, the type of policy offered and perceptions about services are more important. In order to improve the service provided, research in this field is required as some potential customers may regard trustworthy advice, a clear understanding, fair value, personal consideration, dependable performance and continuing service as more important than cost.

ii) *Market Extension*   The market could be extended if sales could be made to existing policy holders (i.e. to encourage the insured to purchase more than one policy).

iii) *Effectiveness of Advertising*   As mentioned earlier, there is little market research information in this field. Perhaps advertisements should be customised to meet the needs of each separate segment, instead of attempting to crowd detailed information about every service into one advertisement. (This is already done by most of the insurance companies in their advertising campaigns.)

Figure 16
Recent and Future Trends in Insura. Marketing[74]

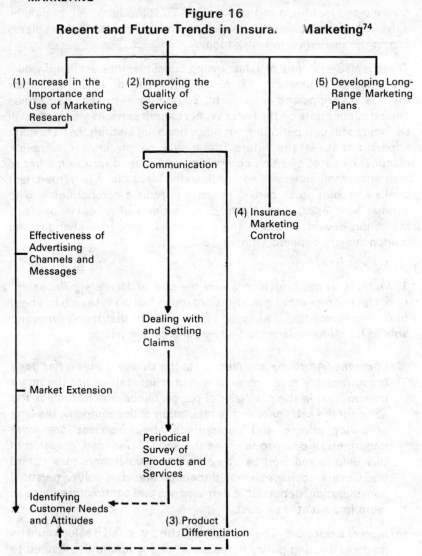

2) *Improving the Quality of Service*

The quality of service should involve not only pre-sales service, but also after-sales service in the form of speed and helpfulness in dealing with claims. The insurer should not quibble over marginal factors in settling claims. Also connected with service improvement is communication in all forms; not only is the promptness of communication vital, but also clarity, accuracy and courtesy of that communication system. This means that today's policy, which is often very lengthy and complicated for a layman, should be simplified and shortened. The effectiveness of communication is important in creating and building up the goodwill of the company. Perhaps each service should be promoted in a separate campaign. In order to improve the quality of service, insurance companies would need:

i) *Research not only into the needs of today but also the needs of tomorrow* Participation from the salesperson is helpful in the creation of new products as it will probably be easier for him to communicate their advantages to his clients.

ii) *Periodical survey on products and services* These should be conducted as insurance policies are usually offered on a long-term basis. Instead of package policies, perhaps the development of variable policies (e.g. life assurance policy or policies with increasing applications) should be looked into, to meet the changing needs of the insured in the face of rapid changes.

3) *Product Differentiation*

Insurance is no exception to the trend towards product diversification. Almost ¾ of all property liability insurance both in the United States and in Western Europe is now written by multiple-line company groups, such as fire and casualty, which historically had been separated.

The implications of this trend are complex. Conceivably, the purposes have varied from better coverage to more convenience and from lower costs to more stable profits. Still, this fundamental assumption that diversification of services in insurance companies is bound to lead to increase in profits *has to be checked*, as it may not be true for all the insurance companies in all the circumstances. Here too, marketing costs analysers might play an important and vital role.

4) *Insurance Marketing Control*

The availability of electronic data processing has already had an important effect on most advanced and aggressive insurance companies. Moreover, because of increasing competition as well as a need to get

more precise and rapid answers to managerial problems, it is
inevitable that an increasing use and application of computerised
techniques will be initiated for controlling marketing performance,
market research, insurance sales forecasting and segmentation of
customers, in order to increase marketing of insurance effectiveness.

5) *Developing Long-Range Marketing Plans*

Most of the leading insurance companies have recently attempted to
develop their long-range marketing plans in order to answer the three
key questions:

 i) what will future markets be like?;

 ii) what will the insurance "product" be?; and,

 iii) how can these markets be reached?

Indeed, the development and implementation of marketing control
techniques have greatly assisted the introduction and application of
planning in insurance marketing.

However, recently in anticipation of the growing complexity of the
market sectors, insurers are now expanding their range of financial
services and are active in mutual funds, equipment leasing, real estate
management, credit financing and related fields. This broadening of
the product spectrum acts as a feedback mechanism and as a positive
reinforcement of the market potential. An important component of the
future marketing environment will probably be a trend towards
integration of insurance and financial services with co-ordinated
benefit planning. The broader product and service needs which are
being identified and the changes which are taking place in insurance
sales methods, should provide a number of advantages for consumers,
including the availability of better advice and simpler 'package'
policies.

Marketing in insurance companies in the 1980's will lead to the
development of insurance holding companies (i.e. the concentration
of the insurance industry into fewer individual companies). These
conglomerates, owned largely by financial and industrial organisations,
will tend to acquire additional "old" insurance companies, attempting
at the same time to diversify the services offered within the financial
sector at large, including personal savings, personal and commercial
finance, mutual funds, equity investments, trust management and
ordinary banking services.

This might lead to certain developments from the insurance sales-person or agent point of view. In particular, the salesperson's profit from selling insurance will grow as a result of a larger variety of insurance products offered, while, on the other hand, the pressure on, and the demands from, the salesperson will increase since the number of insurance companies will be smaller and the competition tougher. With the increase in competition amongst the insurance companies, more of them are increasing their range of automation for more rapid and cheaper direct billing, renewal payment, automatic file maintenance and follow up. IBM already supplies equipment to insurance companies to handle up to 50,000 claims per month at under £18 cost per hour service.

Consumerism and Consumer Protection

Consumerism can be defined as the rising critical awareness by consumers towards the products and services which they consume. As a result, there is an increase in government protectionist legislation and/or consumers' organisation for self defence in the market place (e.g. boycotts, manifestations, advertisements, etc.).

Among the major reasons that have led to the rise of the importance of consumerism are:

i) increasingly educated customers who have come to expect high quality service with the insurance policy which they buy;

ii) inflation, with the inexorable increase in prices, coupled with recession, which has led to the customer becoming more concerned with the quality of products and services; and,

iii) the rising expectations of consumers as a result of advertising and promotional campaigns that are not always fulfilled.

Until very recently, however, the insurance industry has avoided many of the consumerist pressures, mainly because insurance is generally a complex service, little understood by most customers.

Recently, a number of insurance companies (e.g. Siemol Life and Cavendish Life) have become bankrupt leading to some policy holders losing their money. In an effort to protect customers, the U.K. Department of Trade and Industry has now decided to end all marketing by off-shore insurance companies in the U.K. This will be achieved by:

i) prohibiting advertisements by unauthorised insurance companies; and,

ii) prohibiting the solicitation of business by unauthorised insurers.

The off-shore insurance companies were in the past companies registered in the Channel Islands, the Isle of Man, Gibraltar or the West Indies, etc. The various policies offered by them will still be offered to interested customers and market competition thus maintained, but more information about the insurance company and a possible association (and commitment) of a local insurance intermediary will be required.

Consumer protection is necessary because most insurance contracts are highly technical and legal, containing provisions and clauses that might be complex to the average customer. The Government ensures that customers are protected by requiring:

i) reasonable rates (premiums);

ii) adequate and reliable information;

iii) *all* customers who need insurance can have access to insurance arrangements; and,

iv) insurers (insurance companies) are solvent.

In addition, insurance protection laws refer to the taxation issue, the licensing of brokers, agents and agencies, etc. and the formation and operation of insurance companies or agencies. In certain countries, notably the U.S.A. and the U.K., insurance agents and brokers must pass a qualifying examination to obtain a licence. Unfair trade practice (e.g. false advertising or unreasonable "small letter" policies) should be avoided, in order that the insurance buyer will not be misled.

In order to ensure consumer protection many governments operate a number of general strict regulations arising from the legislation:

i) Control over entry into the industry. New entrants are required to have a minimum paid up capital – in the U.K. this is £100,000. In addition, the quality of reinsurance arrangements and the moral standing and past records of the person(s) who act as directors/controllers/managers are taken into account.

ii) Solvency. In order to ensure solvency and consumers' rights, the Government can impose restrictions on the amount of business that an insurance company can accept. The Government might also require details on the valuation of assets, liabilities and other aspects of insurance companies' financial activities.

iii) Insurance companies should present to the relevant authority a "Business Plan" which should include:

a) the company's aims; and,

b) *clear* policy conditions (in order that potential customers will not be misled).

Behind the consumerism movement, there are great opportunities for marketing by insurance companies. If easy contact with the insurance agency and distributor is provided when legitimate customer grievances occur, this will lead to a decrease in customers' dissonance and stronger links between the insurance policy supplier and buyer. Another way to ensure that customers are satisfied is by making sure that advertising and promotional messages are consistent with the quality of services/policies offered. Many insurance buyers are particularly discontented with the "small letters" of their insurance policies. These could be simplified and the opportunity taken to explain the legal terms provided in the policies.

Insurance Marketing Problems and Inflation

Inflation and recession, while major factors in economic discussions, have been given less attention by insurance marketing lecturers and practitioners than, say, new policies (products) development, advertising, insurance salespersons and buyer behaviour, etc. Inflation is, however, not a new phenomenon. Relatively high inflation rates were experienced during and after major wars in many countries, and multi-digit inflation is quite widely spread in certain South American countries.

major impact on the value of life policies at their maturity and the attraction of life insurance policies as "saving for rainy days" diminishes.*

In a number of countries (e.g. Brazil) insurance companies are experimenting with ways to combat the effect of inflation by employing indexed life insurance policies. The use of indexation in Brazil has not, however, resulted in the mitigation of the monetary value erosion produced by inflation, and insurance sales have declined in inflationary periods, whether the life assurance policies were indexed or not. (For a detailed discussion see: Babbel, D.F.: "Inflation Indexation and Life Insurance Sales in Brazil" *The Journal of Risk and Insurance* March 1981, vol. XLVIII, No. 1, pp. 109-135.)

The insurance company should undertake the following steps in order to combat the effects of inflation and recession on its profits and turnover:

i) Promotional price deals (special offer policies) should be used more often and aggressively.

ii) Price increases should be rationalised and explained to the insured (both new and existing customers).

iii) New product development should be undertaken more often, in order to offer a wider variety to all insurance buyers, new and existing customers. Value analyses should be undertaken to reduce the cost of certain policies.

iv) The insurance company should re-examine its distribution channels and favour, wherever possible, low cost distribution channels and intermediaries.

v) The insurance company should attempt to promote and push harder the more profitable policies (products). If necessary, the less profitable, slow turnover policies or agencies should be dropped.

vi) Price discounting and credit facilities should be tightened. Premium reductions can be allowed for advance payment. In order to facilitate quick payment, the insurer can supply the insured with prepaid envelopes or standing orders.

---

* If we imagine that prices increase by a yearly average of 5% and the average life assurance policy extends over 20 years, this means that the money is going to lose about 62% of its value during 20 years:

The price index in 20 years $= (1 + .05)^{20} = 2.65$

Money value index $= \dfrac{1}{2.65} = 0.38$ i.e. the decrease of money value $1 - 0.38 = .62$

CONCLUSIONS

The most important change in insurance marketing today is the recognition by all levels of management of the importance of the marketing concept and that the profitable success of an insurance company depends primarily upon satisfying customer needs. Indeed, insurance, perhaps more than any other product, should rely upon sound marketing practices. It is only through a reasonable sales volume that insurance companies achieve their purpose: predictability of losses and of profits. The control of distribution expenses by insurers, for example, is dependent upon marketing efficiencies, which are (or should be) the result of adjustment to the needs and desires of consumers.

Insurance companies should, therefore, adopt a marketing-orientated approach geared to maximising customer satisfaction. This approach was identified as the insurance marketing programme and consists of five successive stages or elements:

 i) marketing research to identify insurance needs in the market;

 ii) product development to create insurance policies to meet these needs;

 iii) pricing to determine competitive premiums for these policies;

 iv) advertising and promotion to convince potential clients that these policies are best suited to their needs; and,

 v) distribution which involves the selection of appropriate channels through which to sell these policies to customers.

Among these five elements, it has been noted that the final four together comprise what is known as the Insurance Marketing Mix. However, in so far as the insurance marketing mix forms an integral part of the insurance marketing programme, any meaningful analysis of the marketing mix can only take place within the framework of the broader marketing approach. For this reason, one should base any meaningful analysis of marketing in insurance on the insurance marketing programme, marketing strategies and marketing organisation and control.

A detailed examination of each of the five successive stages which make up the insurance marketing programme has been covered in this book. By linking these stages together, it was shown that the marketing programme is a continuous process rather than a collection of independent functions. At one end of the process is the marketing research stage where customer needs are identified and at the other end is the distribution stage where insurance policies are passed on to satisfied customers. Market feedback from the distribution stage (through sales representatives and brokers), and from the preceding advertising and promotion stage (through situation prospecting), revitalises the marketing research stage that regenerates the whole process anew. Thus, the process of insurance marketing (or the insurance marketing programme) as depicted in figure 3 on page 16 is to some extent a self-perpetuating process through the medium of market feedback. However, for continuous effective insurance marketing in a competitive world, the flow of market feedback must be supplemented by a sustained programme of "formal" marketing research.

The existence of various forms of insurance policies available on the market provides sound evidence of the importance of product differentiation and market segmentation in the industry. Their existence also gives expression to the industry's continuous search for new and modified policies having characteristics to meet the needs and wants of policy holders.

Effective selling of policies depends to a large extent on the competence of the salesperson as well as the marketing strategies selected. These should be chosen with care. Some of the qualities to look for in a salesperson are empathy and ego-drive which will enable them to home in on a particular target and sell the policy.

Finally, the marketing of insurance is not static. With the rapid changes in the environment due to advancement in technology and uncertain economic conditions, coupled with inflation, the marketing of insurance will probably be geared more and more towards cost savings techniques.

REFERENCES

1. Eilon, S. and Fowkes, T.R. (eds.): *Applications of Management Science in Banking and Insurance.* Gower Press, 1978.

2. Meidan, A.: *The Marketing of Financial Services — A Bibliographical Pilot Study.* Unpublished working paper, University of Sheffield, December, 1975.

3. "Insurance Advertising", *Campaign* (U.K.), 30th July, 1976.

4. Sequeira, P.: *"The Marketing of Insurance"*, Ph.D. dissertation, University of Sheffield, (forthcoming, 1984), p. 5.

5. Menge, W.O. and Fistner, C.H.: *The Mathematics of Life Insurance,* Macmillan, New York, 1963, p. 49.

6. Bickelhaupt, D.L.: "Trends and Innovations in the Marketing of Insurance", *Business Management,* April, 1976, pp. 16-23.

7. Clayton, G.: "Competition in the Insurance Market 1970-1980", *C.I.I. Monograph Series No. 1* (1981), pp. 1-55.

8. Adelman, W.S.: *"Optimal Operating Volumes and Economies to Scale in the Independent Insurance Agency"*, Ph.D. University of Georgia, 1980, p. 152.

9. Rejda, G.E.: *Principles of Insurance,* Scott, Foresman and Company, Glenview, Illinois, 1982, p. 545.

10. *"Life Assurance and Pensions in the European Community"* — Report by Advanced Study Group No. 200 of the Insurance Institute of London (1975), pp. 22-49.

11. Kotler, P.: *Marketing Management: Analysis, Planning and Control,* fourth edition, Prentice Hall, 1980, p. 29.

12. Brennan, D.B.: "Functional Costs and the Marketing of Life Assurance — A Sketch", *N.A.A. Bulletin,* October, 1960, pp. 61-68.

13. Franklin, P.J. and Woodhead, C.: *"The U.K. Life Assurance Industry"*, Croom Helm Ltd., 1980.

14. Anderson, D.R. and Nevin, J.R.: "Determinants of Young Marrieds' Life Insurance Purchasing Behaviour: A Behavioural Investigation", *Journal of Risk and Insurance,* 1974, pp. 375-386.

15. Dorfman, M.S.: *"The Analysis of the Product Performance of the Life Insurance Industry"*, Ph.D. thesis, 1971, University of Illinois, Urbana, Campaign, U.S.A., pp. 46, 62.

16. Carter, R.L.: *Economics and Insurance,* Ph. Press Ltd., 1979, p. 116.

REFERENCES

17. Haas, A.W. and Berry, L.L.: "Systems S lling of Retail Services", *Bankers' Monthly* (U.S.A.), July, 197& l. 139, pp. 276-283.

18. Meidan, A.: *Bank Marketing Management,* Macmillan series in Marketing, 1984 (in press).

19. Hardin, D.K.: "Marketing Research in Service Industries" in *Handbook of Modern Marketing,* ed. by Buell, V.P., McGraw Hill Book Co., 1964, pp. 56-78.

20. Meidan, A.: "When to Use Nonmetric Multidimensional Scaling in Marketing Research", *European Research,* Vol. 2, March, 1975, pp. 215-227.

21. Kinnear, T.C. and Taylor, J.R.: *Marketing Research: An Applied Approach,* McGraw Hill, U.S.A., 1979.

22. FitzRoy, P.: *Analytical Methods for Marketing Management,* McGraw Hill, U.K., 1976.

23. Wilson, R.M.S. (Ed.): "The Marketing of Financial Services", *Managerial Finance,* Vol. 5, No. 3, 1980, pp. 223-234.

24. Huebner, S.S. and Black, Jr., K.: *Life Insurance, Eighth Edition* Appleton-Century Crofts, 1974.

25. Gartland, P.: "The Quiet Revolution in Life Assurance", *Accountancy,* June, 1979, pp. 79-82.

26. Rudelius W. and Wood G.L.: "Life Insurance Product Innovation", *Journal of Risk and Insurance,* Vol. 37, June, 1970, pp. 169-184.

27. Peterson, R.A. and Rudelius, W., and Wood, G.L.: "Spread of Marketing Innovation in a Service Industry", *Journal of Business,* 19th October, pp. 485-496.

28. Murray, M.: "The Theory and Practice of Innovation in the Private Insurance Business", *Journal of Risk and Business,* December, 1976, pp. 653-672.

29. Kahane, Y.: "Determination of the Product Mix and the Business Policy of an Insurance Company — A Portfolio Approach", *Management Science,* Vol. 23, No. 10, June, 1977, pp. 1060-1069.

30. *"Modern Techniques in the Marketing and Merchandising of Insurance",* Report by Advanced Study Group No. 190, The Insurance Institute of London, 1971.

31. Drake, N.J. and Winton, D.S.: "The Contribution Made by a Marketing Research Programme Towards the Development of a New Major Insurance Product", *European Research,* January, 1977, pp. 34-44.

32. Thomson, H.A.: "The Use of Customer Attitude Assessment in Pricing: An Observation Suggesting the Use of Attitude Questionnaires in the Prices Involving Customer Risk Assessment", *Industrial Marketing Management,* Vol. 4 (1975), No. 2, pp. 107-111.

33. Launie, L.L.: "Price Differentials in Life Insurance", *Journal of Risk and Insurance,* Vol. 35, No. 2, 1968, pp. 283-288.

34. Newman, Seev: "Anticipated and Unanticipated Inflation — Implications to Life Insurance", *Journal of Risk and Insurance,* Vol. 36, No. 3, 1969, pp. 315-319.

35. Brennan, D.B.: "Functional Costs and the Marketing of Life Assurance — A Sketch", *N.A.A. Bulletin,* October, 1960, pp. 61-68.

36. Belth, J.M.: "Deceptive Sales Practice in Life Insurance", *Indiana Business Review,* July-August, 1972, pp. 48-56.

37. Winterbotham, R.W.G.: "Advertising in Insurance", *Policy Holder Insurance Journal,* 18th February, 1972, pp. 293-296.

38. O'Reilly, D.: "When a Little Spending is the Best Policy", *Campaign,* July, 1976, p. 11.

39. "Prospects for Success — The Four General Methods", *The Insurance Mail,* September, 1979, pp. 190-192.

40. Everett, M.: "The Dark Side of Insurance Sales", *Sales and Marketing Management,* February, 1979, pp. 25-29.

41. Kempton, J.A.: "The Role of Life Assurance Salesmen", *Life Assurance — The Challenge of Change Conference,* November, 1975, pp. 129-139.

42. Greenberg, H. and Mayer, D.: "A New Approach to the Scientific Selection of Successful Salesmen", *Journal of Psychology,* 1978, Issue 57, pp. 113-123.

43. Pillsbury, D.: "Identifying the Potentially Successful Salesmen", *Bests' Review (Life/Health Insurance Edition),* May, 1974, pp. 232-234.

44. Greenberg, H.: "MPI Test" in Nordhous, G. and Brown, S.: *Marketing Property and Casualty Insurance,* Insurance Marketing Services of California, Santa Barbara, Cal., U.S.A., 1976.

45. Belth, J.M.: "Deceptive Sales Practices in the Life Insurance Business", *Journal of Risk and Insurance,* Vol. 41, June, 1974, pp. 305-326.

46. Poppleton, S.E. and Lubbock, J.: "Marketing Life Assurance — Cause of Success and Failure in Life Assurance Salesmen", *European Journal of Marketing,* Vol. 11, No. 6, 1977, pp. 418-431.

47. Bieber, R.W.: "Four Tracks for Effective Training Meetings", *Sales Meeting,* July, 1972, pp. 12-17.

48. Waid, C., Clark, D.F., and Ackoff, R.L.: "Allocation of Sales Effort in the Lamp Division of the General Electric Company", *Operations Research,* December, 1956, pp. 629-647.

49. Magee, J.F.: "Determining the Optimum Allocation of Expenditure for Promotional Effort with Operations Research Methods" in *The Frontiers of Marketing Thought and Science* by Bass, F.M. (ed.) American Marketing Association, Chicago, 1958, pp. 215-224.

50. Henry, P.: "Use of the 2-D Principle for Making the Most of Sales Time", *Sales Management* (U.S.A.), May, 1975, pp. 258-260.

51. Meidan, A.: "Sales Force Management", *Management Decision,* December, 1980, Vol. 8, No.8 (Monograph — Special Issue).

52. Meyer, D. and Greenberg, H.M.: "What Makes a Good Salesman?", *Harvard Business Review,* L.V.N., July-August, 1964, pp. 119-125.

53. Wilson, A.: *The Marketing of Services,* Winthrop, 1974, p. 25.

54. Hughes, J.L.: "Expressed Personality Needs as Predictors of Sales Success", *Personnel Psychology,* Vol. IX, 1956, pp. 347-357.

55. Baier, D.E. and Dugan, R.D.: "Factors in Sales Success", *Journal of Applied Psychology,* Vol. XLI, No. 1, 1957, pp. 37-40.

56. Spear, T.W.: *"A Multivariate Analysis of "Self-Concepts" that Might be Related to the Success of Life Insurance Agents",* Ph.D. dissertation, University of Pennsylvania, U.S.A., 1980.

57. Banaka, W.H.: *"A Study of Situational Factors Related to the Performance of Insurance Sales Supervisors",* Ph.D. thesis, University of Houston, 1959, p. 62.

58. Cravens, D.W., Woodruff, R.B. and Stamper, J.C.: "An Analytical Approach for Evaluating Sales Territory Performance", *Journal of Marketing,* January, 1972, Vol. 36, No. 1, pp. 31-37.

59. Vizza, R.F.: "R.O.T.I. Profitable Selling New Maths", *Time and Territory Magazine* (U.S.A.), 2nd May, 1976, pp. 12-21.

60. Adkins, R.T.: "Evaluating and Comparing Salesmen's Performance", *Industrial Marketing Management,* Vol. 8, 1979, pp. 207-212.

61. Etgar, M.: "Service Performance of Insurance Distributors", *Journal of Risk and Insurance,* Vol. 43, No.3, 1976, pp. 487-498.

62. Rubin, H.W. and Zuger, P.A.: "Prospects for Selling Life Insurance Through Retail Banking Outlets", *Journal of Risk and Insurance,* Vol. 42, No. 2, 1975, pp. 303-312.

63. Gee, W.K. and Bird, M.M.: "Insurance Purchasing in the Small Manufacturing Firm", *Journal of Purchasing,* May, 1972, pp. 40-46.

64. Murray, M.L.: "The Theory and Practice of Innovation in the Private Insurance Industry", *Journal of Risk and Insurance,* Vol. 43, December, 1976, pp. 653-672.

65. Thomson, H.A.: "The Use of Customer Attitude Assessment in Pricing. An Observation Suggesting the Use of Attitude Questionnaires in the Pricing of Services Involving Customer Risk Assessment", *Industrial Marketing Management,* 1975, Vol. 4, No. 4, pp. 107-111.

66. Dugdale, I.: "Corporate Planning and Control Systems in Williams and Glyn's Bank", *Long Range Planning,* Vol. 11, October, 1978, pp. 41-46.

67. Ansoff, H.I.: *Corporate Strategy,* Pelican, 1979.

68. Katz, R.L.: *Cases and Concepts in Corporate Stategy,* Prentice Hall, 1977.

69. Clayton, G.: *British Insurance,* Elek Books, London, 1971.

70. Meidan, A.: *"The Appraisal of Managerial Performance"* American Management Association (Bibliography and Review Series), November, 1981, A.M.A., New York.

71. Alexander, R.S.: "The Death and Burial of Sick Products", *Journal of Marketing,* Vol. 28, April, 1969, p. 1.

72. Schwarzschild, S. and Zubay, E.A.: *Principles of Life Insurance,* (Vol. II) — Richard Irwin Inc., Homewood, Illinois, 1977.

73. Dowsett, R.C., Lusk, W.B. and Darrow, P.M.: "Three Views of Life Insurance Marketing in the Future", *Best's Review (Life/Health Edition),* March, 1974, pp. 20-22, 77-81.

REFERENCES

74. Meidan, A.: "Marketing for Insurance Companies in Britain — The State of the Art", *The Journal of Insurance Issues and Practices* (U.S.A.), Vol. 3, 1979, No. 1, pp. 17-28.

INDEX

A

Actuarial, 46, 49, 60, 67
Advertising, 5, 11-12, 15, 16, 36, 46, 71-79
  channels of, 71-72
  effectiveness, 32, 137-138
  functions of, 71-74
  institutional, 136
  life assurances, 78-79
  media (see also Advertising channels), 20, 32, 76-77
  themes, 32
  to consumers, 20, 32
  to trade, 20
  to students, 30
Agency, 49
Agents, (see also Distribution channels), 9, 83-86
  advice, 36, 38, 40, 85
  and marketing strategy, 85-86
  characteristics, 36, 38, 40
  commissions, 5, 82, 89
  exclusive, 83-85
  friendliness, 36
  independent, 83-84
  in Japan, 30
  in the USA, 30
  own case, 20
  part-time, 20
  service (see also Services), 22, 85
Anderson, D.R., 19
Assurance, (see also Life assurance),
  markets, 43
  purchasing behaviour, 19
  sales, 8, 18
  term, 44-45
Automation, 119, 135-141
Automobile insurance, (see also Motor insurance), 32

B

Babbel, D.F., 144
Banks, 4, 6, 30, 47, 87, 88-89
Behaviour, 12, 18, 22, 24-25
  characteristics, 19
Berry, L.L., 27
Bickelhaupt D.L., 86
Bieber, R.W., 98
Boston Consulting Group, 50-52
Brand,
  names, 20
  preference standing, 21
Brennan, D.B., 65
Brokers, 16, 18, 20, 30, 82-83, 87-89
  commissions, 45, 89
Building societies, vii, 4, 6, 18, 87
Buying,
  processes, 26-27
  styles, 25

C

Carter, R.L., 65
Channels of distribution, (see Distribution channels),
Claims, 46, 59, 65-66
Class rating, 62-64
Commercial Union, 60
Competition, 5, 7, 11, 12, 20, 43
Consumerism, 141-143
Control, 17, 62, 125-133, 139-140
  methods of, 128-130
  objectives of, 128
  over entry, (see Consumer protection)
Correlation, 33, 35-37, 40
  Spearman, 36-38
Costing, 61-62, 135
  functional, 17
  operational, 59, 81
Cravens, D.W., 111

Customers, (see also Insurance
customers),
  behaviour, (see also Behaviour),
    17-24, 32, 41
  characteristics, 24
  life styles, 3, 28
  needs, 16-17, 23, 25, 43, 137-
    138
  perceptions, 24
  preferences, 16, 20
  protection, 49, 141-143
  satisfaction, viii, 3, 9-11, 12

D

Direct mail, 33-34. 72-74, 81-83
Distribution channels, 3, 11-12, 15,
  17, 19, 81-91
  advantages of, (see also Agents),
    86
  direct, 16, 81-86
    by association, 83, 86
    by company's staff, 82-84
  for life assurance, 88-90
  indirect, 16, 83, 86-90
    advantages of, 83 86-87
    home service, 83, 88
    part-time, 83, 88

E

Effectiveness research
  (see Research for Effectiveness
  and also Performing) 34, 83, 123
Endowment, ix, 44, 46
Environment, 12, 17

F

Financial
  customers, 27
  Fishbein's formula, 21
  FitzRoy, P., 34
  forecasting, 11
  institutions, viii
  markets, 19
  needs, 23
  services, v

G

Gifts, 36, 40
Government, 12, 49, 62
  insurance, 5
  restrictions, 45
Greenberg, H., 95, 104

H

Haas, A.W., 27
Hazards, 2, 4, 21, 23, 50
Health insurance, 32
Hospital insurance (see also
  insurance-medical), 48

I

Income, 15, 43
Inflation, 40, 48, 52, 59, 61, 68,
  143-145
  effects of, 7-8, 20, 36
  indexed, 144
Insurance, (see also Life and
  Assurance),
  agents (see Agents)
  attitudes to, 23
  channels (see Distribution
    channels)
  characteristics, 1-8
  companies, 1, 5-7, 9-10, 12, 35,
    46-47
  customers, (see also Customers),
    1, 7, 19
  demand of, 2, 19
  distribution (see Distribution
    channels)
  home contents, 4, 55
  in the UK, vii, ix, 4-5, 30, 55
  in the USA, vii, ix, 1, 5, 23, 32,
    47, 55, 60, 139
  liability, viii
  life, (see Life and also Assurance),
    viii
  marine, 48
  marketing, (see also Marketing),
    vii-viii, 1, 2
  medical, (see also Hospital
    insurance) 4, 48, 56-57

objectives, vii-viii, 28
organisations, (see also
   Organisation), 12
pecuniary, viii
performance (see Performance)
personal, 1-2, 5
planning of (see also Planning),
   52, 77-78, 121-123
policy (see Policy)
premiums (see Premium)
products, (see Products and also
   Segmentation), 8, 12, 27, 32,
   34
property, viii, 48
rate, (see Rate making)
selection of, 36-37, 40-41
service, (see Service), 1-2, 24,
   28, 31, 53, 57
Insuremanship, 5
Insurers, 1, 5, 19, 29-30, 52-53
   characteristics, 12
   evaluation of, 23
   selection of, 23
Interviews-in-depth, 21
Investment, 44

J

Judgment rating, 63, 65

K

Kinnear, T.C., 34
Kotler, P.J., 119

L

Legal and General Assurance
   Society, 89
Legislation, 6, 50, 55
Life (see Insurance life and also
   Assurance)
   assurances, (see Assurance and
      also Insurance), 6-7, 17-18,
      43, 45-49
   companies, 18, 45
   cycle (see also Segmentation), 27
   industrial, 17, 45
   insurance (see also Insurance
      and Life assurance), 4, 6-7

offices, 18
ordinary, 17, 45
policies, ix, 19, 55
reasons for buying, 22
Loss, 62
frequency of, 21
incidence, vii
pooling, 5, 52
ratio, 63-64
size of, 21
Loyalty, 30

M

Management, 67
Marine insurance, 65
Market
   definition of, 26
   segmentation, (see also
      Segmentation), 17-30
   share, 32
Marketing, (see also Insurance
   marketing)
   approach, (see also Marketing
      concept), 10-11
   concept, (see also Marketing
      approach), 9-12
   feedback, 16
   management, v, 31
   mix, 1, 12, 15-16, 19-20, 33, 53
   orientation, 12
   procedures, 19, 136-137
   programme, 12, 15-17, 43
   research, (see also Market
      research), 11-12, 15-16, 21,
      25, 31-41, 43, 59, 137-139
   strategy, (see Strategy)
Market research, (see also Marketing
   research)
   experiments, 33-39
   for effectiveness, 32-33
   objectives of, 31
   questions, 33
   studies, 31-34
   techniques of, 31-34
Mass Merchandising, (see
   Merchandising)

Meidan, A., 102, 112
Merchandising, 8, 33, 86, 90-91
Merit rating, 63-65
Messages, 20, 32
Methods
    multivariate, 34
    univariate, 34
Meyer, D., 104
Mortality, 65-68
Mortgage repayment, 18, 22
Motor insurance, (see also Auto-
    mobile insurance), 1, 4, 28, 48,
    55, 62

N

Nevin, J. R., 9
New products, (see also Products)
    in insurance, 34

O

O'Reilly, D., 74
Organisation, (see also Sales
    organisation and Insurance
    organisation), 125-133
    by functions, 125-127
    of marketing department, 125-
    127
    of sales (see Sales organisation)

P

Pensions, 17-18, 43
Performance, (see also Salesforce
    performance), 130-133
Planning, (see also Products
    planning and also Insurance
    planning), 77-78, 140
Policy, (see also Insurance policy
    and also Products), 1, 9, 11, 15,
    17, 21, 35, 45-48, 54
    benefits, 23
    cancellation of, 36-38
    cost, 66
    features, 15
    flexibility, 36-38, 40-41
    holder, 7, 47-48, 67-69
    package, 8, 20, 43, 53

preference for, 21, 39
    quality of, 23
    redeemability, 15, 22
    surrender value, 7
    time horizon, 36-38, 40
    value of, 21
Preferences, 21
    attributes for, 21
Premium, (see also Pricing), v, 5-6,
    8, 11, 15, 17, 20, 36, 40, 43-46,
    59-60, 67-68
    gross annual, 20, 68
    level of, 20, 68
    net single, 20, 46, 68
    systems, 68-69
Pricing, (see also Rate making), 1-3,
    11-12, 15, 19, 28, 32, 49, 59-69
    and competition, 59
    and inflation, 59
    comparison, 5
    competitive, 61-62
    differentials, 60-61
    discriminatory, 60
    full cost, 65
    objectives, 59-61
    of life assurances, 65-69
    policy, 7, 61
    strategy, (see also Strategy), 60
    tactics, 50
Probability, 28
Products, (see also Insurance
    products), 11, 27
    characteristics, 1-5, 43, 46
    conventional, 20, 44-45
    design, 49
    development, 3, 12, 15, 20, 43-
    57
    differentiation, 43, 45, 48-49,
    139
    innovation, (see also Products,
    new) 5, 10, 46-49
    life cycle, 18, 49-54
    mix, 53
    new, 34, 46-49, 135
    package, 5
    planning, (see also Planning) 15

variants/variety, 2, 36, 44-46
Profitability, 31, 36, 40-41, 52, 59-60
Promotion, 3, 11-12, 15-16, 19, 71-79
   channels of, 72-73
   goals of, 74-75
   response to, 25
   to brokers, 79
   tools, 20
Prospecting, 16, 31, 74-78, 82
Protection, viii, 18, 44, 50
   to family, 22
   to old age, 22

Q

Questionnaires, 21, 33, 35-36, 61

R

Ratemaking, (see also Pricing), 8, 61-65
   objectives of, 62
   types of, 62-65
Real estate, 48
Redeemability, (see also Value of surrender), 15, 46
Regulations, 49-50, 87
Reinsurance, 49, 87
Rejda, G.E., 5
Research, (see Marketing research, and also Market research), 11
Retirement income, 18
Risks, 2-3, 8, 30-31, 49-50, 67
   analysis of, 24
   attitudes to, 21
   future of, 23
   management of, 48
   natural, 2-3
   of default, 22, 46
   reappraisal of, 24
   sharing, 12
   social, 2-3
   technical, 2-3
   transfer 5, 19

S

Sales
   concept, 9-10

organisation, (see Organisation and also Insurance organisations) 17
   orientation, 10, 12
   presentation, 28
Salesforce, (see also Salespersons), 93-112
   feedback, 17
   functions, 93, 94
   selection, 94-97
   training, 94, 97-99
   organisation, (see also Organisation), 97
   performance, (see also Performance), 102-112
      determinants, 104-108
      methods of evaluating, 108-112
      via agency development, 103
      via sales maintenance, 103
   supervision 99-102
      methods, 100-102
      of new accounts, 101-102
Salespersons, (see also Salesforce) 5, 16, 20
   incentives to, 45, 101-102
   skills, 94-97
   tasks, 90
   turnover, 94
Segmentation, 17-30, 32, 37
   and customer types, 25
   bases for, 22
   by education (see also Students), 19
   by household income, 19, 29
   by life cycle, 27-28
   by life offices, 17
   conditions for, 26
   demographic, 18, 28-29, 82
   effective, 26
   factors for, 18
   geographic, 29, 82
   of young married couples, 18
   other forms of, 29
      students, 30
      women, 29-30

psychographic, 28, 82
social class, 28-29
types of, 27
Selling, (see also Distribution
  channels), 1, 28
  by mail, 20
  by part-time agents, 20
  direct, 20, 34
  indirect, 20
  techniques, 8-9, 12
Sequeira, P., 2
Service(s), (see also Insurance
  service), 53, 138-139
  at time of claims, 24
  before sale, 24
  contract, 24, 47
  development, (see Product
    development
  during contract, 24, 36
  offered, 20, 27, 56
  quasi-collective, viii, 12
Simulation, 33
Spear, T. W., 105
Stamper, J. C., 111
Standard Life, 89
Strategies, 32, 34, 46, 48, 115-123
  in product development, 54-57
  of competition, 119-121
  of growth, 116-119
  selection of, 41, 120-121
Students, (see also Segmentation,
  other forms of), 30, 35-41
Sun Alliance, 53-54

T

Taylor, J. R., 34
Tax, 43-45, 52, 62
  allowance, 20, 36-40
  clawback, 40
  concessions, 6
Trade unions, 18
Training (see Salesforce training)

U

Uncertainty, 2, 31, 52

Underwriting, 8, 47, 62, 135

V

Value
  of surrender, (see also
    Redeemability), 36, 40, 45-46
Variables, 35-36, 38-39, 41
Vizza, R.F., 111

W

Wilson, R.M.S., 104
Winterbottom, 73
Women, (see also Segmentation,
  other forms of)
  as agents, 95
  roles in insurance, 29-30
  services to, 29-30
Woodruff, R.B., 111